ROMAN MISSAL

A Study Text with Excerpts
from the New English Translation

NOT FOR LITURGICAL USE

ROMAN MISSAL

EXCERPTS FROM THE ENGLISH LANGUAGE EDITION
OF THE ROMAN MISSAL

FOR STUDY PURPOSES ONLY

VOX CLARA COMMITTEE
CONGREGATION FOR DIVINE WORSHIP
AND THE DISCIPLINE OF THE SACRAMENTS
VATICAN CITY

A.D. MMXI

ISBN 978-1-936045-40-2

www.theologicalforum.org

GENERAL INDEX

Presentation 7
Editorial Note 8
The General Instruction of the Roman Missal (Excerpts) 9

ORDER OF MASS

The Order of Mass 15
Prefaces
    Preface I of Advent 35
    Preface II of Advent 36
    Preface I of the Sundays in Ordinary Time. 37
    Preface II of the Sundays in Ordinary Time 38
Eucharistic Prayers
    Eucharistic Prayer I (The Roman Canon) 40
    Eucharistic Prayer II 48
    Eucharistic Prayer III 52
    Eucharistic Prayer IV 57
The Communion Rite 63
The Concluding Rites 68

PROPER OF TIME

Advent
    First Sunday of Advent 72
    Second Sunday of Advent 74
    Third Sunday of Advent 75
    Fourth Sunday of Advent. 76
Christmas Time
    The Nativity of the Lord 77
    The Holy Family of Jesus, Mary and Joseph 85
    Solemnity of Mary, Mother of God. 87
    Second Sunday after the Nativity 89
    The Epiphany of the Lord 90
    The Baptism of the Lord 94

Lent
    First Sunday of Lent 98
    Second Sunday of Lent 100
    Third Sunday of Lent 102
    Fourth Sunday of Lent. 104
    Fifth Sunday of Lent 106
Easter Time
    Easter Sunday of the Resurrection of the Lord 109
    Second Sunday of Easter (or of Divine Mercy) 112
    Third Sunday of Easter 114
    Fourth Sunday of Easter 116
    Fifth Sunday of Easter. 117
    Sixth Sunday of Easter 118
    Seventh Sunday of Easter 119

PROPER OF SAINTS

November 121

MASSES AND PRAYERS
FOR VARIOUS NEEDS AND OCCASIONS

I. For Holy Church
    1. For the Church 150

VOTIVE MASSES

13. Saint Joseph 158

CONGREGATION FOR DIVINE WORSHIP
AND THE DISCIPLINE OF THE SACRAMENTS

PRESENTATION

The great challenge of our generation is not just to ensure correct and dignified liturgical celebration according to the approved forms, but to be open in a spirit of prayer to the great mysteries of our redemption in Christ that the liturgy makes present ever anew. Only by this authentic assimilation of the mystery will we become truly Christian and so achieve the salvation that Christ lives in our midst to bring us.

It is with these thoughts in mind that I welcome with joy and appreciation this book, which makes available substantial extracts from the new English translation of the Roman Missal. The thanks of the Congregation for Divine Worship and the Discipline of the Sacraments goes out to the publishing house, Midwest Theological Forum, as also to the Vox Clara Committee for having made arrangements for this initiative.

The new Missal is the fruit of the labors of many, in the first place of the Bishops of the English-speaking world, with whom the prime responsibility lies for the preparation of the text. It has been heartening to see the commitment of the Bishops to this particular project, whose importance the Holy Father Benedict XVI stressed in a recent discourse, saying that: *"Through these sacred texts and the actions that accompany them, Christ will be made present and active in the midst of his people."*

Numerous initiatives are currently being undertaken to fulfill *"the task of preparing for the reception of the new translation by clergy and lay faithful."* As Pope Benedict has said, *"Many will find it hard to adjust to unfamiliar texts after nearly forty years of continuous use of the previous translation. The change will need to be introduced with due sensitivity, and the opportunity for catechesis that it presents will need to be firmly grasped. I pray that in this way any risk of confusion or bewilderment will be averted, and the change will serve instead as a springboard for a renewal and a deepening of Eucharistic devotion all over the English-speaking world."*

The publication of this book of extracts aims simply at furthering this aim. As is clear from its form, it is not destined for liturgical use but for careful study and meditation. The Bishops and their helpers are already hard at work preparing worthy liturgical editions of all the texts of the new English Missal. In the meantime this little publication offers a preview of major parts of the Order of Mass and a short selection from other parts of the Missal, including many ancient prayers now rendered in dignified, pastorally accessible and theologically and spiritually rich English.

I gladly make my own the wish expressed by the Holy Father that *"As the prayers of God's people rise before him like incense (cf. Psalm 140:2), may the Lord's blessing come down upon all who have contributed their time and expertise to crafting the texts in which those prayers are expressed."*

By divine grace, may this publication make its own real contribution to achieving a fruitful conclusion to such a vital undertaking.

From the Vatican,
9 September 2010

Aɴᴛᴏɴɪᴏ Cᴀʀᴅ. Cᴀñɪᴢᴀʀᴇꜱ Lʟᴏᴠᴇʀᴀ
Prefect

EDITIORIAL NOTE

The Church makes careful provision for the adaptation of the Roman Missal by Conferences of Bishops in order that the celebration of the Sacred Liturgy "may correspond all the more fully to the norms and the spirit of the sacred Liturgy…"[1]

This Study Edition provides a selection of texts from the common English translation approved and confirmed for use in all territories where English is spoken.[2] There are several ways, however, in which ritual editions of the *Roman Missal* to be published in various territories will differ from this common text:

General Instruction of the Roman Missal

The adaptation of certain paragraphs of the *General Instruction of the Roman Missal*, within the competence of particular Conferences of Bishops,[3] will be given within the text of the each Conference's edition of the *Roman Missal*. This Study Edition refers only to the original, unadapted Latin text of the General Instruction.

Antiphons and Other Chants

Because the translation of scripturally based texts should "be guided by the manner of expression that is characteristic of the version of the Sacred Scriptures approved for liturgical use in the territories for which the translation is being prepared,"[4] the antiphons and other chants based on Scripture texts in this Edition have been revised to reflect the vocabulary and manner of expression of the biblical translations approved for liturgical use in the dioceses of the United States of America.[5] The Congregation has indicated to all other Conferences of Bishops its willingness to consider for the *recognitio* other translations of the antiphons and other chants which similarly reflect the biblical translations approved and confirmed for use in the Liturgy in their particular territories.

Particular Calendars and Propers

The particular calendar and propers of individual Conferences of Bishops are not included in this Study Edition. Approved and confirmed editions of each of these texts are regularly to be found in the editions published for a given territory. Certain additional adaptations to the Order of Mass or other parts of the *Roman Missal* which have been confirmed for particular Conferences of Bishops are not included in this Study Edition.

---

[1] *General Instruction of the Roman Missal* [GIRM], no. 386.
[2] Cf. GIRM, nos. 389 and 392.
[3] GIRM, no. 390. This provision applies particularly to GIRM, nos. 43, 273, 48, 74, 87, 362, 82, 160, 283, 301, 326, 329, 339, and 342–346.
[4] Congregation for Divine Worship and the Discipline of the Sacraments, Instruction *Liturgiam authenticam* (28 March 2001), no. 49.
[5] The approved and confirmed English-language translations of the Scriptures for the dioceses of the United States of America are the New American Bible and Conception Grail Psalter.

THE GENERAL INSTRUCTION
OF THE ROMAN MISSAL
(Excerpts)

CHAPTER II
THE STRUCTURE OF THE MASS, ITS ELEMENTS AND ITS PARTS

I. THE GENERAL STRUCTURE OF THE MASS

27. At Mass or the Lord's Supper the People of God is called together, with a Priest presiding and acting in the person of Christ, to celebrate the memorial of the Lord or Eucharistic Sacrifice.[37] In an outstanding way there applies to such a local gathering of the holy Church the promise of Christ: "Where two or three are gathered in my name, there am I in their midst" (*Mt* 18:20). For in the celebration of Mass, in which the Sacrifice of the Cross is perpetuated,[38] Christ is really present in the very assembly gathered in his name, in the person of the minister, in his word, and indeed substantially and uninterruptedly under the Eucharistic species.[39]

28. The Mass consists in some sense of two parts, namely the Liturgy of the Word and the Liturgy of the Eucharist, these being so closely interconnected that they form but one single act of worship.[40] For in the Mass is spread the table both of God's word and of the Body of Christ, and from it the faithful are to be instructed and refreshed.[41] There are also certain rites that open and conclude the celebration.

II. THE DIFFERENT ELEMENTS OF THE MASS

Reading and Explaining the Word of God

29. When the Sacred Scriptures are read in the Church, God himself speaks to his people, and Christ, present in his word, proclaims the Gospel.

Therefore, the readings from the word of God are to be listened to reverently by everyone, for they are an element of the greatest importance in the Liturgy. Although in the readings from Sacred Scripture the word of God is addressed to all people of whatever era, and is understandable to them, a fuller understanding and a greater

---

[37] Cf. Second Ecumenical Council of the Vatican, Decree on the Ministry and Life of Priests, *Presbyterorum ordinis*, no. 5; Constitution on the Sacred Liturgy, *Sacrosanctum Concilium*, no. 33.

[38] Cf. Ecumenical Council of Trent, Session XXII, *Doctrina de ss. Missæ sacrificio*, cap. 1: Denzinger-Schönmetzer, no. 1740; Paul VI, Solemn Profession of Faith, 30 June 1968, no. 24: *Acta Apostolicæ Sedis* 60 (1968) p. 442.

[39] Cf. Second Ecumenical Council of the Vatican, Constitution on the Sacred Liturgy, *Sacrosanctum Concilium*, no. 7; Paul VI, Encyclical Letter *Mysterium fidei*, 3 September 1965: *Acta Apostolicæ Sedis* 57 (1965) p. 764; Sacred Congregation of Rites, Instruction *Eucharisticum mysterium*, 25 May 1967, no. 9: *Acta Apostolicæ Sedis* 59 (1967) p. 547.

[40] Cf. Second Ecumenical Council of the Vatican, Constitution on the Sacred Liturgy, *Sacrosanctum Concilium*, no. 56; Sacred Congregation of Rites, Instruction *Eucharisticum mysterium*, 25 May 1967, no. 3: *Acta Apostolicæ Sedis* 59 (1967) p. 542.

[41] Cf. Second Ecumenical Council of the Vatican, Constitution on the Sacred Liturgy, *Sacrosanctum Concilium*, nos. 48, 51; Dogmatic Constitution on Divine Revelation, *Dei Verbum*, no. 21; Decree on the Ministry and Life of Priests, *Presbyterorum ordinis*, no. 4.

efficaciousness of the word is nevertheless fostered by a living commentary on the word, that is, by the Homily, as part of the liturgical action.[42]

The Prayers and Other Parts Pertaining to the Priest

30.   Among those things assigned to the Priest, the prime place is occupied by the Eucharistic Prayer, which is the high point of the whole celebration. Next are the orations, that is to say, the Collect, the Prayer over the Offerings, and the Prayer after Communion. These prayers are addressed to God by the Priest who presides over the assembly in the person of Christ, in the name of the entire holy people and of all present.[43] Hence they are rightly called the "presidential prayers".

31.   Likewise it is also for the Priest, in the exercise of his office of presiding over the gathered assembly, to offer certain explanations that are foreseen in the rite itself. Where this is laid down by the rubrics, the celebrant is permitted to adapt them somewhat so that they correspond to the capacity for understanding of those participating. However, the Priest should always take care to keep to the sense of the explanatory text given in the Missal and to express it in just a few words. It is also for the presiding Priest to regulate the word of God and to impart the final blessing. He is permitted, furthermore, in a very few words, to give the faithful an introduction to the Mass of the day (after the initial Greeting and before the Penitential Act), to the Liturgy of the Word (before the readings), and to the Eucharistic Prayer (before the Preface), though never during the Eucharistic Prayer itself; he may also make concluding comments regarding the entire sacred action before the Dismissal.

32.   The nature of the "presidential" parts requires that they be spoken in a loud and clear voice and that everyone listen to them attentively.[44] Therefore, while the Priest is pronouncing them, there should be no other prayers or singing, and the organ or other musical instruments should be silent.

33.   For the Priest, as the one who presides, expresses prayers in the name of the Church and of the assembled community; but at times he prays only in his own name, asking that he may exercise his ministry with greater attention and devotion. Prayers of this kind, which occur before the reading of the Gospel, at the Preparation of the Gifts, and also before and after the Communion of the Priest, are said quietly.

Other Formulas Occurring during the Celebration

34.   Since the celebration of Mass by its nature has a "communitarian" character,[45] both the dialogues between the Priest and the assembled faithful, and the acclamations are of great significance;[46] for they are not simply outward signs of communal celebration but foster and bring about communion between Priest and people.

[42] Cf. Second Ecumenical Council of the Vatican, Constitution on the Sacred Liturgy, *Sacrosanctum Concilium*, nos. 7, 33, 52.

[43] Cf. *ibidem*, no. 33.

[44] Cf. Sacred Congregation of Rites, Instruction *Musicam sacram*, 5 March 1967, no. 14: *Acta Apostolicæ Sedis* 59 (1967) p. 304.

[45] Cf. Second Ecumenical Council of the Vatican, Constitution on the Sacred Liturgy, *Sacrosanctum Concilium*, nos. 26–27; Sacred Congregation of Rites, Instruction *Eucharisticum mysterium*, 25 May 1967, no. 3d: *Acta Apostolicæ Sedis* 59 (1967) p. 542.

35. The acclamations and the responses of the faithful to the Priest's greetings and prayers constitute that level of active participation that is to be made by the assembled faithful in every form of the Mass, so that the action of the whole community may be clearly expressed and fostered.[47]

36. Other parts, most useful for expressing and fostering the active participation of the faithful, and which are assigned to the whole gathering, include especially the Penitential Act, the Profession of Faith, the Universal Prayer, and the Lord's Prayer.

37. Finally, among other formulas:

a) Some constitute an independent rite or act, such as the *Gloria in excelsis* (*Glory to God in the highest*), the Responsorial Psalm, the *Alleluia* and verse before the Gospel, the *Sanctus* (*Holy, Holy, Holy*), the Memorial Acclamation, and the chant after Communion;

b) Others, on the other hand, accompany some other rite, such as the chants at the Entrance, at the Offertory, at the fraction (*Agnus Dei*, *Lamb of God*) and at Communion.

The Manner of Pronouncing the Different Texts

38. In texts that are to be pronounced in a loud and clear voice, whether by the Priest or the deacon, or by a reader, or by everyone, the voice should correspond to the genre of the text itself, that is, depending upon whether it is a reading, a prayer, an explanatory comment, an acclamation, or a sung text; it should also be suited to the form of celebration and to the solemnity of the gathering. Consideration should also be given to the characteristics of different languages and of the culture of different peoples.

Therefore, in the rubrics and in the norms that follow, words such as "say" and "proclaim" are to be understood either of singing or of reciting, with due regard for the principles stated here above.

The Importance of Singing

39. The Christian faithful who come together as one in expectation of the Lord's coming are instructed by the Apostle Paul to sing together Psalms, hymns, and spiritual canticles (cf. *Col* 3:16). Singing is the sign of the heart's joy (cf. *Acts* 2:46). Thus St Augustine says rightly, "Singing is for one who loves",[48] and there is also an ancient proverb: "Whoever sings well prays twice over."

40. Great importance should therefore be attached to the use of singing in the celebration of the Mass, with due consideration for the culture of peoples and abilities of each liturgical assembly. Although it is not always necessary (e.g., in weekday Masses) to sing all the texts that are in principle meant to be sung, every care should be taken that singing by the ministers and the people not be absent in celebrations that occur on Sundays and on Holydays of Obligation.

[46] Cf. Second Ecumenical Council of the Vatican, Constitution on the Sacred Liturgy, *Sacrosanctum Concilium*, no. 30.

[47] Cf. Sacred Congregation of Rites, Instruction *Musicam sacram*, 5 March 1967, no. 16a: *Acta Apostolicæ Sedis* 59 (1967) p. 305.

[48] St Augustine of Hippo, *Sermo* 336, 1: PL 38: 1472.

However, in the choosing of the parts actually to be sung, preference is to be given to those that are of greater importance and especially to those which are to be sung by the Priest or the deacon or a reader, with the people replying, or by the Priest and people together.[49]

41.   The main place should be given, all things being equal, to Gregorian chant, as being proper to the Roman Liturgy. Other kinds of sacred music, in particular polyphony, are in no way excluded, provided that they correspond to the spirit of the liturgical action and that they foster the participation of all the faithful.[50]

Since the faithful from different countries come together ever more frequently, it is desirable that they know how to sing together at least some parts of the Ordinary of the Mass in Latin, especially the Profession of Faith and the Lord's Prayer, according to the simpler settings.[51]

Gestures and Bodily Posture

42.   The gestures and bodily posture of both the Priest, the deacon, and the ministers, and also of the people, must be conducive to making the entire celebration resplendent with beauty and noble simplicity, to making clear the true and full meaning of its different parts, and to fostering the participation of all.[52] Attention must therefore be paid to what is determined by this General Instruction and by the traditional practice of the Roman Rite and to what serves the common spiritual good of the People of God, rather than private inclination or arbitrary choice.

A common bodily posture, to be observed by all those taking part, is a sign of the unity of the members of the Christian community gathered together for the sacred Liturgy, for it expresses the intentions and spiritual attitude of the participants and also fosters them.

43.   The faithful should stand from the beginning of the Entrance chant, or while the Priest approaches the altar, until the end of the Collect; for the *Alleluia* chant before the Gospel; while the Gospel itself is proclaimed; during the Profession of Faith and the Universal Prayer; and from the invitation, *Orate, fratres* (**Pray, brethren**), before the Prayer over the Offerings until the end of Mass, except at the places indicated here below.

The faithful should sit, on the other hand, during the readings before the Gospel and the Responsorial Psalm and for the Homily and during the Preparation of the Gifts at the Offertory; and, if appropriate, during the period of sacred silence after Communion.

They should kneel, on the other hand, at the Consecration, except when prevented on occasion by ill health, or for reasons of lack of space, of the large number of

[49] Cf. Sacred Congregation of Rites, Instruction *Musicam sacram*, 5 March 1967, nos. 7, 16: *Acta Apostolicæ Sedis* 59 (1967), pp. 302, 305.

[50] Cf. Second Ecumenical Council of the Vatican, Constitution on the Sacred Liturgy, *Sacrosanctum Concilium*, no. 116; cf. also no. 30.

[51] Cf. Second Ecumenical Council of the Vatican, Constitution on the Sacred Liturgy, *Sacrosanctum Concilium*, no. 54; Sacred Congregation of Rites, Instruction *Inter Oecumenici*, 26 September 1964, no. 59: *Acta Apostolicæ Sedis* 56 (1964) p. 891; Instruction *Musicam sacram*, 5 March 1967, no. 47: *Acta Apostolicæ Sedis* 59 (1967) p. 314.

people present, or for another reasonable cause. However, those who do not kneel ought to make a profound bow when the Priest genuflects after the Consecration.

It is for the Conference of Bishops, in accordance with the norm of law, to adapt the gestures and bodily postures described in the Order of Mass to the culture and reasonable traditions of peoples.[53] However, attention must be paid to ensuring that such adaptations correspond to the meaning and character of each part of the celebration. Where it is the practice for the people to remain kneeling after the *Sanctus* (*Holy, Holy, Holy*) until the end of the Eucharistic Prayer and before Communion when the Priest says *Ecce Agnus Dei* (*This is the Lamb of God*), it is laudable for this practice to be retained.

For the sake of uniformity in gestures and bodily postures during one and the same celebration, the faithful should follow the instructions which the deacon, a lay minister, or the Priest gives, according to what is laid down in the Missal.

44.   Among gestures are included also actions and processions, by which the Priest, with the deacon and ministers, goes to the altar; the deacon carries the Evangeliary or Book of Gospels to the ambo before the proclamation of the Gospel; the faithful bring up the gifts and come forward to receive Communion. It is appropriate that actions and processions of this sort be carried out with decorum while the chants proper to them are sung, in accordance with the norms laid down for each.

Silence

45.   Sacred silence also, as part of the celebration, is to be observed at the designated times.[54] Its nature, however, depends on the moment when it occurs in the different parts of the celebration. For in the Penitential Act and again after the invitation to pray, individuals recollect themselves; whereas after a reading or after the Homily, all meditate briefly on what they have heard; then after Communion, they praise God in their hearts and pray to him.

Even before the celebration itself, it is a praiseworthy practice for silence to be observed in the church, in the sacristy, in the vesting room, and in adjacent areas, so that all may dispose themselves to carry out the sacred celebration in a devout and fitting manner.

---

[52] Cf. Second Ecumenical Council of the Vatican, Constitution on the Sacred Liturgy, *Sacrosanctum Concilium*, nos. 30, 34; cf. also no. 21.

[53] Cf. *ibidem*, no. 40; Congregation for Divine Worship and the Discipline of the Sacraments, Instruction *Varietates legitimæ*, 25 January 1994, no. 41: *Acta Apostolicæ Sedis* 87 (1995) p. 304.

[54] Cf. Second Ecumenical Council of the Vatican, Constitution on the Sacred Liturgy, *Sacrosanctum Concilium*, no. 30; Sacred Congregation of Rites, Instruction *Musicam sacram*, 5 March 1967, no. 17: *Acta Apostolicæ Sedis* 59 (1967) p. 305.

THE ORDER OF MASS

The Introductory Rites

1.   When the people are gathered, the Priest approaches the altar with the ministers while the Entrance Chant is sung.

When he has arrived at the altar, after making a profound bow with the ministers, the Priest venerates the altar with a kiss and, if appropriate, incenses the cross and the altar. Then, with the ministers, he goes to the chair.

THE INTRODUCTORY RITES

The rites that precede the Liturgy of the Word, namely, the Entrance, the Greeting, the Penitential Act, the *Kyrie*, the *Gloria in excelsis* (**Glory to God in the highest**) and Collect, have the character of a beginning, an introduction, and a preparation.

Their purpose is to ensure that the faithful who come together as one, establish communion and dispose themselves properly to listen to the word of God and to celebrate the Eucharist worthily.

In certain celebrations that are combined with Mass according to the norms of the liturgical books, the Introductory Rites are omitted or take place in a particular way. (*The General Instruction of the Roman Missal* [GIRM], no. 46)

The Entrance

When the people are gathered, and as the Priest enters with the deacon and ministers, the Entrance Chant begins. Its purpose is to open the celebration, foster the unity of those who have been gathered, introduce their thoughts to the mystery of the liturgical time or festivity, and accompany the procession of the Priest and ministers. (GIRM, no. 47)

The Entrance Chant

This chant is sung alternately by the choir and the people or similarly by a cantor and the people, or entirely by the people, or by the choir alone. It is possible to use the antiphon with its Psalm from the *Graduale Romanum* or the *Graduale Simplex*, or another chant that is suited to the sacred action, the day, or the time of year (Cf. John Paul II, Apostolic Letter *Dies Domini*, 31 May 1998, no. 50: *Acta Apostolicæ Sedis* 90 (1998), p. 745), and whose text has been approved by the Conference of Bishops.

If there is no singing at the Entrance, the antiphon given in the Missal is recited either by the faithful, or by some of them, or by a reader; otherwise, it is recited by the Priest himself, who may even adapt it as an introductory explanation (*cf. no. 31*). (GIRM, no. 48)

Reverence to the Altar

When they have arrived at the sanctuary, the Priest, the deacon, and the ministers reverence the altar with a profound bow.

Moreover, as an expression of veneration, the Priest and deacon then kiss the altar itself; the Priest, if appropriate, also incenses the cross and the altar. (GIRM, no. 49)

When the Entrance Chant is concluded, the Priest and the faithful, standing, sign themselves with the Sign of the Cross, while the Priest, facing the people, says:

In the name of the Father, and of the Son, and of the Holy Spirit.

The people reply:

Amen.

2.   Then the Priest, extending his hands, greets the people, saying:

The grace of our Lord Jesus Christ,
and the love of God,
and the communion of the Holy Spirit
be with you all.

Or:

Grace to you and peace from God our Father
and the Lord Jesus Christ.

Or:

The Lord be with you.

The people reply:

And with your spirit.

In this first greeting a Bishop, instead of **The Lord be with you**, says:

Peace be with you.

3.   The Priest, or a Deacon, or another minister, may very briefly introduce the faithful to the Mass of the day.

Greeting of the Assembled People

When the Entrance Chant is concluded, the Priest stands at the chair and, together with the whole gathering, signs himself with the Sign of the Cross. Then by means of the Greeting he signifies the presence of the Lord to the assembled community. By this greeting and the people's response, the mystery of the Church gathered together is made manifest.

After the greeting of the people, the Priest, or the deacon, or a lay minister may very briefly introduce the faithful to the Mass of the day. (GIRM, no. 50)

Notes

Penitential Act*

4.   Then follows the Penitential Act, to which the Priest invites the faithful, saying:

Brethren (brothers and sisters), let us acknowledge our sins,
and so prepare ourselves to celebrate the sacred mysteries.

A brief pause for silence follows. Then all recite together the formula of general confession:

I confess to almighty God
and to you, my brothers and sisters,
that I have greatly sinned,
in my thoughts and in my words,
in what I have done and in what I have failed to do,

And, striking their breast, they say:

through my fault, through my fault,
through my most grievous fault;

Then they continue:

therefore I ask blessed Mary ever-Virgin,
all the Angels and Saints,
and you, my brothers and sisters,
to pray for me to the Lord our God.

---

  * From time to time on Sundays, especially in Easter Time, instead of the customary Penitential Act, the blessing and sprinkling of water may take place (as in Appendix II, pp. 000–000) as a reminder of Baptism.

The Penitential Act

After this, the Priest calls upon the whole community to take part in the Penitential Act, which, after a brief pause for silence, it does by means of a formula of general confession. The rite concludes with the Priest's absolution, which, however, lacks the efficacy of the Sacrament of Penance.

From time to time on Sundays, especially in Easter Time, instead of the customary Penitential Act, the blessing and sprinkling of water may take place as a reminder of Baptism. (GIRM, no. 51)

The absolution by the Priest follows:
**May almighty God have mercy on us,
forgive us our sins,
and bring us to everlasting life.**

The people reply:
Amen.

Or:

5.   The Priest invites the faithful to make the Penitential Act:
**Brethren (brothers and sisters), let us acknowledge our sins,
and so prepare ourselves to celebrate the sacred mysteries.**

A brief pause for silence follows.

The Priest then says:
Have mercy on us, O Lord.

The people reply:
For we have sinned against you.

The Priest:
Show us, O Lord, your mercy.

The people:
And grant us your salvation.

The absolution by the Priest follows:
**May almighty God have mercy on us,
forgive us our sins,
and bring us to everlasting life.**

The people reply:
Amen.

Or:

6.   The Priest invites the faithful to make the Penitential Act:
**Brethren (brothers and sisters), let us acknowledge our sins,
and so prepare ourselves to celebrate the sacred mysteries.**

A brief pause for silence follows.

The Priest, or a Deacon or another minister, then says the following or other invocations with Kyrie, eleison (Lord, have mercy):

You were sent to heal the contrite of heart:

Lord, have mercy.   Or: **Kyrie, eleison.**

The people reply:

Lord, have mercy.   Or: **Kyrie, eleison.**

The Priest:

You came to call sinners:

Christ, have mercy.   Or: **Christe, eleison.**

The people:

Christ, have mercy.   Or: **Christe, eleison.**

The Priest:

You are seated at the right hand of the Father to intercede for us:

Lord, have mercy.   Or: **Kyrie, eleison.**

The people:

Lord, have mercy.   Or: **Kyrie, eleison.**

The absolution by the Priest follows:

May almighty God have mercy on us,
forgive us our sins,
and bring us to everlasting life.

The people reply:

Amen.

---

7.   The **Kyrie eleison (Lord, have mercy)** invocations follow, unless they have just occurred in a formula of the Penitential Act.

The Kyrie Eleison

After the Penitential Act, the *Kyrie, eleison* (*Lord, have mercy*), is always begun, unless it has already been part of the Penitential Act. Since it is a chant by which the faithful acclaim the Lord and implore his mercy, it is usually executed by everyone, that is to say, with the people and the choir or cantor taking part in it.

Each acclamation is usually pronounced twice, though it is not be excluded that it be repeated several times, by reason of the character of the various languages, as well as of the artistry of the music or of other circumstances. When the *Kyrie* is sung as a part of the Penitential Act, a trope precedes each acclamation. (GIRM, no. 52)

℣. **Lord, have mercy.**   ℟. **Lord, have mercy.**

℣. **Christ, have mercy.**   ℟. **Christ, have mercy.**

℣. **Lord, have mercy.**   ℟. **Lord, have mercy.**

Or:

℣. **Kyrie, eleison.**   ℟. **Kyrie, eleison.**

℣. **Christe, eleison.**   ℟. **Christe, eleison.**

℣. **Kyrie, eleison.**   ℟. **Kyrie, eleison.**

8.   Then, when it is prescribed, this hymn is either sung or said:

Glory to God in the highest,
and on earth peace to people of good will.

We praise you,
we bless you,
we adore you,
we glorify you,
we give you thanks for your great glory,
Lord God, heavenly King,
O God, almighty Father.

Lord Jesus Christ, Only Begotten Son,
Lord God, Lamb of God, Son of the Father,
you take away the sins of the world,
       have mercy on us;
you take away the sins of the world,
       receive our prayer;
you are seated at the right hand of the Father,
       have mercy on us.

The Gloria in Excelsis

The *Gloria in excelsis* (*Glory to God in the highest*) is a most ancient and venerable hymn by which the Church, gathered in the Holy Spirit, glorifies and entreats God the Father and the Lamb. The text of this hymn may not be replaced by any other. It is intoned by the Priest or, if appropriate, by a cantor or by the choir; but it is sung either by everyone together, or by the people alternately with the choir, or by the choir alone. If not sung, it is to be recited either by everybody together or by two choirs responding one to the other.

It is sung or said on Sundays outside Advent and Lent, and also on Solemnities and Feasts, and at particular celebrations of a more solemn character. (GIRM, no. 53)

For you alone are the Holy One,
you alone are the Lord,
you alone are the Most High,
Jesus Christ,
with the Holy Spirit,
in the glory of God the Father.
Amen.

9.   When this hymn is concluded, the Priest, with hands joined, says:

Let us pray.

And all pray in silence with the Priest for a while.

Then the Priest, with hands extended, says the Collect prayer, at the end of which the people acclaim:

Amen.

The Collect
Next the Priest calls upon the people to pray and everybody, together with the Priest, observes a brief silence so that they may become aware of being in God's presence and may call to mind their intentions. Then the Priest pronounces the prayer usually called the Collect and through which the character of the celebration finds expression. By an ancient tradition of the Church, the Collect prayer is usually addressed to God the Father, through Christ, in the Holy Spirit (Cf. Tertullian, *Adversus Marcionem*, IV, 9: CCSL 1, p. 560; Origen, *Disputatio cum Heracleida*, no. 4, 24: *Sources chrétiennes* 67, p. 62; *Statuta Concilii Hipponensis Breviata*, no. 21: CCSL 149, p. 39), and is concluded with a Trinitarian ending, or longer ending… (GIRM, no. 54)

The Liturgy of the Word

10. Then the reader goes to the ambo and reads the First Reading, while all sit and listen.

To indicate the end of the reading, the reader acclaims:

The word of the Lord.

All reply:

Thanks be to God.

THE LITURGY OF THE WORD

The main part of the Liturgy of the Word is made up of the readings from Sacred Scripture together with the chants occurring between them. As for the Homily, the Profession of Faith and the Universal Prayer, they develop and conclude it. For in the readings, as explained by the Homily, God speaks to his people (Cf. Second Ecumenical Council of the Vatican, Constitution on the Sacred Liturgy, *Sacrosanctum Concilium*, no. 33), opening up to them the mystery of redemption and salvation, and offering spiritual nourishment; and Christ himself is present through his word in the midst of the faithful (Cf. *ibidem*, no. 7). By silence and by singing, the people make this divine word their own, and affirm their adherence to it by means of the Profession of Faith; finally, having been nourished by the divine word, the people pour out their petitions by means of the Universal Prayer for the needs of the whole Church and for the salvation of the whole world. (GIRM, no. 55)

Silence

The Liturgy of the Word is to be celebrated in such a way as to favor meditation, and so any kind of haste such as hinders recollection is clearly to be avoided. In the course of it, brief periods of silence are also appropriate, accommodated to the assembled congregation; by means of these, under the action of the Holy Spirit, the word of God may be grasped by the heart and a response through prayer may be prepared. It may be appropriate to observe such periods of silence, for example, before the Liturgy of the Word itself begins, after the First and Second Reading, and lastly at the conclusion of the Homily (Cf. Missale Romanum, *Ordo lectionum Missæ*, editio typica altera, 1981, no. 28). (GIRM, no. 56)

The Biblical Readings

In the readings, the table of God's word is spread before the faithful, and the treasures of the Bible are opened to them (Cf. Second Ecumenical Council of the Vatican, Constitution on the Sacred Liturgy, *Sacrosanctum Concilium*, no. 51). Hence, it is preferable that the arrangement of the biblical readings be maintained, for by them the unity of both Testaments and of salvation history is brought out. Nor is it lawful to replace the readings and Responsorial Psalm, which contain the word of God, with other, non-biblical texts (Cf. John Paul II, Apostolic Letter *Vicesimus quintus annus*, 4 December 1988, no. 13: *Acta Apostolicæ Sedis* 81 (1989), p. 910). (GIRM, no. 57)

11. The psalmist or cantor sings or says the Psalm, with the people making the response.

12. After this, if there is to be a Second Reading, a reader reads it from the ambo, as above.

To indicate the end of the reading, the reader acclaims:

The word of the Lord.

All reply:

Thanks be to God.

13. There follows the Alleluia or another chant laid down by the rubrics, as the liturgical time requires.

The Responsorial Psalm

After the First Reading follows the Responsorial Psalm, which is an integral part of the Liturgy of the Word and which has great liturgical and pastoral importance, since it fosters meditation on the word of God.

The Responsorial Psalm should correspond to each reading and should usually be taken from the Lectionary.

It is preferable for the Responsorial Psalm to be sung, at least as far as the people's response is concerned. Hence the psalmist or cantor of the Psalm, sings the Psalm verses at the ambo or another suitable place, while the whole congregation sits and listens, normally taking part by means of the response, except when the Psalm is sung straight through, that is, without a response. However, in order that the people may be able to sing the Psalm response more easily, texts of some responses and Psalms have been chosen for the different times of the year or for the different categories of Saints. These may be used instead of the text corresponding to the reading whenever the Psalm is sung. If the Psalm cannot be sung, then it should be recited in a way that is particularly suited to fostering meditation on the word of God.

Instead of the Psalm assigned in the Lectionary, there may be sung either the responsorial Gradual from the *Graduale Romanum*, or the Responsorial Psalm or the *Alleluia* Psalm from the *Graduale Simplex*, as described in these books. (GIRM, no. 61)

The Acclamation before the Gospel

After the reading that immediately precedes the Gospel, the *Alleluia* or another chant laid down by the rubrics is sung, as the liturgical time requires. An acclamation of this kind constitutes a rite or act in itself, by which the gathering of the faithful welcome and greet the Lord who is about to speak to them in the Gospel and profess their faith by means of the chant. It is sung by everybody, standing, and is led by the choir or a cantor, being repeated as the case requires. The verse, on the other hand, is sung either by the choir or by a cantor… (GIRM, no. 62)

THE LITURGY OF THE WORD

14. Meanwhile, if incense is used, the Priest puts some into the thurible. After this, the Deacon who is to proclaim the Gospel, bowing profoundly before the Priest, asks for the blessing, saying in a low voice:

Your blessing, Father.

The Priest says in a low voice:

May the Lord be in your heart and on your lips,
that you may proclaim his Gospel worthily and well,
in the name of the Father and of the Son ✠ and of the Holy Spirit.

The Deacon signs himself with the Sign of the Cross and replies:

Amen.

If, however, a Deacon is not present, the Priest, bowing before the altar, says quietly:

Cleanse my heart and my lips, almighty God,
that I may worthily proclaim your holy Gospel.

15. The Deacon, or the Priest, then proceeds to the ambo, accompanied, if appropriate, by ministers with incense and candles. There he says:

The Lord be with you.

The people reply:

And with your spirit.

The Deacon, or the Priest:

A reading from the holy Gospel according to N.

and, at the same time, he makes the Sign of the Cross on the book and on his forehead, lips, and breast.

The people acclaim:

Glory to you, O Lord.

Then the Deacon, or the Priest, incenses the book, if incense is used, and proclaims the Gospel.

16. At the end of the Gospel, the Deacon, or the Priest, acclaims:

The Gospel of the Lord.

All reply:

Praise to you, Lord Jesus Christ.

Then he kisses the book, saying quietly:

Through the words of the Gospel
may our sins be wiped away.

17. Then follows the Homily, which is to be preached by a Priest or Deacon on all Sundays and Holydays of Obligation; on other days, it is recommended.

18. At the end of the Homily, the Symbol or Profession of Faith or Creed, when prescribed, is either sung or said:

I believe in one God,
the Father almighty,
maker of heaven and earth,
of all things visible and invisible.

I believe in one Lord Jesus Christ,
the Only Begotten Son of God,
born of the Father before all ages.
God from God, Light from Light,
true God from true God,
begotten, not made, consubstantial with the Father;
through him all things were made.
For us men and for our salvation
he came down from heaven,

At the words that follow, up to and including **and became man**, all bow.

and by the Holy Spirit was incarnate of the Virgin Mary,
and became man.

The Homily

The Homily is part of the Liturgy and is highly recommended (Cf. Second Ecumenical Council of the Vatican, Constitution on the Sacred Liturgy, *Sacrosanctum Concilium*, no. 52; *Code of Canon Law*, can. 767 § 1), for it is necessary for the nurturing of the Christian life. It should be an explanation of some aspect of the readings from Sacred Scripture or of another text from the Ordinary or the Proper of the Mass of the day and should take into account both the mystery being celebrated and the particular needs of the listeners (Cf. Sacred Congregation of Rites, Instruction *Inter Œcumenici*, 26 September 1964, no. 54: *Acta Apostolicæ Sedis* 56 (1964), p. 890). (GIRM, no. 65)

The Profession of Faith

The purpose of the Creed or Profession of Faith, is that the whole gathered people may respond to the word of God proclaimed in the readings taken from Sacred Scripture and explained in the Homily and that they may also honor and confess the great mysteries of the faith by pronouncing the rule of faith in a formula approved for liturgical use and before the celebration of these mysteries in the Eucharist begins. (GIRM, no. 67)

For our sake he was crucified under Pontius Pilate,
he suffered death and was buried,
and rose again on the third day
in accordance with the Scriptures.

He ascended into heaven
and is seated at the right hand of the Father.
He will come again in glory
to judge the living and the dead
and his kingdom will have no end.

I believe in the Holy Spirit, the Lord, the giver of life,
who proceeds from the Father and the Son,
who with the Father and the Son is adored and glorified,
who has spoken through the prophets.

I believe in one, holy, catholic and apostolic Church.
I confess one Baptism for the forgiveness of sins
and I look forward to the resurrection of the dead
and the life of the world to come. Amen.

19.   Instead of the Niceno-Constantinopolitan Creed, especially during Lent and Easter
Time, the baptismal Symbol of the Roman Church, known as the Apostles' Creed, may
be used.

I believe in God,
the Father almighty,
Creator of heaven and earth,
and in Jesus Christ, his only Son, our Lord,

At the words that follow, up to and including the Virgin Mary, all bow.

who was conceived by the Holy Spirit,
born of the Virgin Mary,
suffered under Pontius Pilate,
was crucified, died and was buried;
he descended into hell;
on the third day he rose again from the dead;
he ascended into heaven,
and is seated at the right hand of God the Father almighty;
from there he will come to judge the living and the dead.

I believe in the Holy Spirit,
the holy catholic Church,
the communion of saints,
the forgiveness of sins,
the resurrection of the body,
and life everlasting. Amen.

20. Then follows the Universal Prayer, that is, the Prayer of the Faithful or Bidding Prayers.

The Universal Prayer

In the Universal Prayer or Prayer of the Faithful, the people respond in some sense to the word of God which they have received in faith and, exercising the office of their baptismal priesthood, offer prayers to God for the salvation of all. It is desirable that there usually be such a form of prayer in Masses celebrated with the people, so that petitions may be offered for holy Church, for those who govern with authority over us, for those weighed down by various needs, for all humanity, and for the salvation of the whole world (Cf. Second Ecumenical Council of the Vatican, Constitution on the Sacred Liturgy, *Sacrosanctum Concilium*, no. 53). (GIRM, no. 69)

The Liturgy of the Eucharist

21. When all this has been done, the Offertory Chant begins. Meanwhile, the ministers place the corporal, the purificator, the chalice, the pall, and the Missal on the altar.

22. It is desirable that the faithful express their participation by making an offering, bringing forward bread and wine for the celebration of the Eucharist and perhaps other gifts to relieve the needs of the Church and of the poor.

THE LITURGY OF THE EUCHARIST

At the Last Supper Christ instituted the Paschal Sacrifice and banquet, by which the Sacrifice of the Cross is continuously made present in the Church whenever the Priest, representing Christ the Lord, carries out what the Lord himself did and handed over to his disciples to be done in his memory (Cf. Second Ecumenical Council of the Vatican, Constitution on the Sacred Liturgy, *Sacrosanctum Concilium*, no. 47; Sacred Congregation of Rites, Instruction *Eucharisticum mysterium*, 25 May 1967, no. 3a, b: *Acta Apostolicæ Sedis* 59 (1967), pp. 540–541). (GIRM, no. 72)

For Christ took the bread and the chalice, gave thanks, broke the bread and gave it to his disciples, saying, Take, eat and drink: this is my Body; this is the chalice of my Blood. Do this in memory of me. Hence, the Church has arranged the entire celebration of the Liturgy of the Eucharist in parts corresponding to precisely these words and actions of Christ, namely:

a) At the Preparation of the Gifts, bread and wine with water are brought to the altar, the same elements, that is to say, which Christ took into his hands.

b) In the Eucharistic Prayer, thanks is given to God for the whole work of salvation, and the offerings become the Body and Blood of Christ.

c) Through the fraction and through Communion, the faithful, though many, receive from the one bread the Lord's Body and from the one chalice the Lord's Blood in the same way that the Apostles received them from the hands of Christ himself.

The Preparation of the Gifts

At the beginning of the Liturgy of the Eucharist the gifts which will become Christ's Body and Blood are brought to the altar.

First of all, the altar or Lord's table, which is the center of the whole Liturgy of the Eucharist (Cf. Sacred Congregation of Rites, Instruction *Inter Œcumenici*, 26 September 1964, no. 91: *Acta Apostolicæ Sedis* 56 (1964), p. 898; Instruction *Eucharisticum mysterium*, 25 May 1967, no. 24: *Acta Apostolicæ Sedis* 59 (1967), p. 554), is made ready when on it are placed the corporal, purificator, Missal and chalice (unless this last is prepared at the credence table).

The offerings are then brought forward. It is a praiseworthy practice for the bread and wine to be presented by the faithful. They are then accepted at an appropriate place by the Priest or the deacon to be carried to the altar. Even though the faithful no longer bring from their own possessions the bread and wine intended for the liturgy as was once the case, nevertheless the rite of carrying up the offerings still keeps its spiritual efficacy and significance.

Even money or other gifts for the poor or for the Church, brought by the faithful or collected in the church, are acceptable; given their purpose they are to be put in a suitable place away from the Eucharistic table. (GIRM, no. 73)

23.   The Priest, standing at the altar, takes the paten with the bread and holds it slightly raised above the altar with both hands, saying in a low voice:

Blessed are you, Lord God of all creation,
for through your goodness we have received
the bread we offer you:
fruit of the earth and work of human hands,
it will become for us the bread of life.

Then he places the paten with the bread on the corporal.

If, however, the Offertory Chant is not sung, the Priest may speak these words aloud; at the end, the people may acclaim:

Blessed be God for ever.

24.   The Deacon, or the Priest, pours wine and a little water into the chalice, saying quietly:

By the mystery of this water and wine
may we come to share in the divinity of Christ
who humbled himself to share in our humanity.

25.   The Priest then takes the chalice and holds it slightly raised above the altar with both hands, saying in a low voice:

Blessed are you, Lord God of all creation,
for through your goodness we have received
the wine we offer you:
fruit of the vine and work of human hands,
it will become our spiritual drink.

Then he places the chalice on the corporal.

Presentation of the Gifts

The procession bringing the gifts is accompanied by the Offertory chant (*cf. no. 37 b*), which continues at least until the gifts have been placed on the altar. The norms on the manner of singing are the same as for the Entrance chant (*cf. no. 48*). Singing may always accompany the rite at the offertory, even when there is no procession with the gifts. (GIRM, no. 74)

Placing Gifts on the Altar

The bread and wine are placed on the altar by the Priest to the accompaniment of the prescribed formulas; the Priest may incense the gifts placed on the altar and then incense the cross and the altar itself, so as to signify the Church's offering and prayer rising like incense in the sight of God. Next, the Priest, because of his sacred ministry, and the people, by reason of their baptismal dignity, may be incensed by the deacon or by another minister. (GIRM, no. 75)

If, however, the Offertory Chant is not sung, the Priest may speak these words aloud; at the end, the people may acclaim:

Blessed be God for ever.

26. After this, the Priest, bowing profoundly, says quietly:

With humble spirit and contrite heart
may we be accepted by you, O Lord,
and may our sacrifice in your sight this day
be pleasing to you, Lord God.

27. If appropriate, he also incenses the offerings, the cross, and the altar. A Deacon or other minister then incenses the Priest and the people.

28. Then the Priest, standing at the side of the altar, washes his hands, saying quietly:

Wash me, O Lord, from my iniquity
and cleanse me from my sin.

29. Standing at the middle of the altar, facing the people, extending and then joining his hands, he says:

Pray, brethren (brothers and sisters),
that my sacrifice and yours
may be acceptable to God,
the almighty Father.

The people rise and reply:

May the Lord accept the sacrifice at your hands
for the praise and glory of his name,
for our good
and the good of all his holy Church.

30. Then the Priest, with hands extended, says the Prayer over the Offerings, at the end of which the people acclaim:

Amen.

Washing of Hands

Then the Priest washes his hands at the side of the altar, a rite in which the desire for interior purification finds expression. (GIRM, no. 76)

The Prayer over the Offerings

Once the offerings have been placed on the altar and the accompanying rites completed, by means of the invitation to pray with the Priest and by means of the Prayer over the Offerings, the Preparation of the Gifts is concluded and preparation made for the Eucharistic Prayer... (GIRM, no. 77)

THE EUCHARISTIC PRAYER

31. Then the Priest begins the Eucharistic Prayer.

Extending his hands, he says:

The Lord be with you.

The people reply:

And with your spirit.

The Priest, raising his hands, continues:

Lift up your hearts.

The people:

We lift them up to the Lord.

The Priest, with hands extended, adds:

Let us give thanks to the Lord our God.

The people:

It is right and just.

The Priest, with hands extended, continues the Preface.

The Eucharistic Prayer

Now the center and high point of the entire celebration begins, namely, the Eucharistic Prayer itself, that is, the prayer of thanksgiving and sanctification. The Priest calls upon the people to lift up their hearts towards the Lord in prayer and thanksgiving; he associates the people with himself in the Prayer that he addresses in the name of the entire community to God the Father through Jesus Christ in the Holy Spirit. Furthermore, the meaning of this Prayer is that the whole congregation of the faithful joins with Christ in confessing the great deeds of God and in the offering of Sacrifice. The Eucharistic Prayer requires that everybody listens to it with reverence and in silence. (GIRM, no. 78)

The main elements of which the Eucharistic Prayer consists may be distinguished from one another in this way:

a) The *thanksgiving* (expressed especially in the Preface), in which the Priest, in the name of the whole of the holy people, glorifies God the Father and gives thanks to him for the whole work of salvation or for some particular aspect of it, according to the varying day, festivity, or time of year.

At the end of the Preface he joins his hands and concludes the Preface with the people, singing or saying aloud:

Holy, Holy, Holy Lord God of hosts.
Heaven and earth are full of your glory.
Hosanna in the highest.
Blessed is he who comes in the name of the Lord.
Hosanna in the highest.

Or:

Sanctus, Sanctus, Sanctus Dóminus Deus Sábaoth.
Pleni sunt cæli et terra glória tua.
Hosánna in excélsis.
Benedíctus qui venit in nómine Dómini.
Hosánna in excélsis.

---

b) The *acclamation*, by which the whole congregation, joining with the heavenly powers, sings the *Sanctus* (*Holy, Holy, Holy*). This acclamation, which constitutes part of the Eucharistic Prayer itself, is pronounced by all the people with the Priest.

c) The *epiclesis*, in which, by means of particular invocations, the Church implores the power of the Holy Spirit that the gifts offered by human hands be consecrated, that is, become Christ's Body and Blood, and that the unblemished sacrificial Victim to be consumed in Communion may be for the salvation of those who will partake of it.

d) The *Institution narrative and Consecration*, by which, by means of the words and actions of Christ, that Sacrifice is effected which Christ himself instituted during the Last Supper, when he offered his Body and Blood under the species of bread and wine, gave them to the Apostles to eat and drink, and leaving with the latter the command to perpetuate this same mystery.

32. In all Masses, the Priest celebrant is permitted to sing parts of the Eucharistic Prayer provided with musical notation below, pp.**000ff.**, especially the principal parts.

In Eucharistic Prayer I, the Roman Canon, the words included in brackets may be omitted.

e) The *anamnesis*, by which the Church, fulfilling the command that she received from Christ the Lord through the Apostles, celebrates the memorial of Christ, recalling especially his blessed Passion, glorious Resurrection and Ascension into heaven.

f) The *oblation*, by which, in this very memorial, the Church, in particular that gathered here and now, offers the unblemished sacrificial Victim in the Holy Spirit to the Father. The Church's intention, indeed, is that the faithful not only offer this unblemished sacrificial Victim but also learn to offer their very selves (Cf. Second Ecumenical Council of the Vatican, Constitution on the Sacred Liturgy, *Sacrosanctum Concilium*, no. 48; Sacred Congregation of Rites, Instruction *Eucharisticum mysterium*, 25 May 1967, no. 12: *Acta Apostolicæ Sedis* 59 (1967), pp. 548–549), and so day by day to be brought, through the mediation of Christ, into unity with God and with each other, so that God may at last be all in all (Cf. Second Ecumenical Council of the Vatican, Constitution on the Sacred Liturgy, *Sacrosanctum Concilium*, no. 48; Decree on the Ministry and Life of Priests, *Presbyterorum ordinis*, no. 5; Sacred Congregation of Rites, Instruction *Eucharisticum mysterium*, 25 May 1967, no. 12: *Acta Apostolicæ Sedis* 59 (1967), pp. 548–549).

g) The *intercessions*, by which expression is given to the fact that the Eucharist is celebrated in communion with the whole Church, of both heaven and of earth, and that the oblation is made for her and for all her members, living and dead, who are called to participate in the redemption and salvation purchased by the Body and Blood of Christ.

h) The *concluding doxology*, by which the glorification of God is expressed and which is affirmed and concluded by the people's acclamation *Amen*. (GIRM, no. 79)

PREFACE I OF ADVENT
The two comings of Christ

33. The following Preface is said in Masses of Advent from the First Sunday of Advent to 16 December and in other Masses that are celebrated in Advent and have no proper Preface.

It is truly right and just, our duty and our salvation,
always and everywhere to give you thanks,
Lord, holy Father, almighty and eternal God,
through Christ our Lord.

For he assumed at his first coming
the lowliness of human flesh,
and so fulfilled the design you formed long ago,
and opened for us the way to eternal salvation,
that, when he comes again in glory and majesty
and all is at last made manifest,
we who watch for that day
may inherit the great promise
in which now we dare to hope.

And so, with Angels and Archangels,
with Thrones and Dominions,
and with all the hosts and Powers of heaven,
we sing the hymn of your glory,
as without end we acclaim:

Holy, Holy, Holy Lord God of hosts...

PREFACE II OF ADVENT
The twofold expectation of Christ

34.   The following Preface is said in Masses of Advent from 17 December to 24 December and in other Masses that are celebrated in Advent and have no proper Preface.

It is truly right and just, our duty and our salvation,
always and everywhere to give you thanks,
Lord, holy Father, almighty and eternal God,
through Christ our Lord.

For all the oracles of the prophets foretold him,
the Virgin Mother longed for him
with love beyond all telling,
John the Baptist sang of his coming
and proclaimed his presence when he came.

It is by his gift that already we rejoice
at the mystery of his Nativity,
so that he may find us watchful in prayer
and exultant in his praise.

And so, with Angels and Archangels,
with Thrones and Dominions,
and with all the hosts and Powers of heaven,
we sing the hymn of your glory,
as without end we acclaim:

Holy, Holy, Holy Lord God of hosts...

Notes

PREFACE I OF THE SUNDAYS IN ORDINARY TIME
The Paschal Mystery and the People of God

52. The following Preface is said on Sundays in Ordinary Time.

It is truly right and just, our duty and our salvation,
always and everywhere to give you thanks,
Lord, holy Father, almighty and eternal God,
through Christ our Lord.

For through his Paschal Mystery,
he accomplished the marvelous deed,
by which he has freed us from the yoke of sin and death,
summoning us to the glory of being now called
a chosen race, a royal priesthood,
a holy nation, a people for your own possession,
to proclaim everywhere your mighty works,
for you have called us out of darkness
into your own wonderful light.

And so, with Angels and Archangels,
with Thrones and Dominions,
and with all the hosts and Powers of heaven,
we sing the hymn of your glory,
as without end we acclaim:

Holy, Holy, Holy Lord God of hosts . . .

PREFACE II OF THE SUNDAYS IN ORDINARY TIME
The mystery of salvation

53.　The following Preface is said on Sundays in Ordinary Time.

It is truly right and just, our duty and our salvation,
always and everywhere to give you thanks,
Lord, holy Father, almighty and eternal God,
through Christ our Lord.

For out of compassion for the waywardness that is ours,
he humbled himself and was born of the Virgin;
by the passion of the Cross, he freed us from unending death,
and by rising from the dead, he gave us life eternal.

And so, with Angels and Archangels,
with Thrones and Dominions,
and with all the hosts and Powers of heaven,
we sing the hymn of your glory,
as without end we acclaim:

Holy, Holy, Holy Lord God of hosts…

EUCHARISTIC PRAYERS

EUCHARISTIC PRAYER I
(THE ROMAN CANON)

83. ℣. The Lord be with you.
℟. And with your spirit.

℣. Lift up your hearts.
℟. We lift them up to the Lord.

℣. Let us give thanks to the Lord our God.
℟. It is right and just.

Then follows the Preface to be used in accord with the rubrics, which concludes:

Holy, Holy, Holy Lord God of hosts.
Heaven and earth are full of your glory.
Hosanna in the highest.
Blessed is he who comes in the name of the Lord.
Hosanna in the highest.

84. The Priest, with hands extended, says:

To you, therefore, most merciful Father,
we make humble prayer and petition
through Jesus Christ, your Son, our Lord:

He joins his hands and says

that you accept

He makes the Sign of the Cross once over the bread and chalice together, saying:

and bless ✠ these gifts, these offerings,
these holy and unblemished sacrifices,

With hands extended, he continues:

which we offer you firstly
for your holy catholic Church.
Be pleased to grant her peace,
to guard, unite and govern her
throughout the whole world,
together with your servant N. our Pope
and N. our Bishop,*
and all those who, holding to the truth,
hand on the catholic and apostolic faith.

---

   * Mention may be made here of the Coadjutor Bishop, or Auxiliary Bishops, as noted in the *General Instruction of the Roman Missal*, no. 149.

85. Commemoration of the Living.

Remember, Lord, your servants N. and N.

The Priest joins his hands and prays briefly for those for whom he intends to pray.

Then, with hands extended, he continues:

and all gathered here,
whose faith and devotion are known to you.
For them, we offer you this sacrifice of praise
or they offer it for themselves
and all who are dear to them:
for the redemption of their souls,
in hope of health and well-being,
and paying their homage to you,
the eternal God, living and true.

86. Within the Action.

In communion with those whose memory we venerate,
especially the glorious ever-Virgin Mary,
Mother of our God and Lord, Jesus Christ,
† and blessed Joseph, her Spouse,
your blessed Apostles and Martyrs,
Peter and Paul, Andrew,
(James, John,
Thomas, James, Philip,
Bartholomew, Matthew,
Simon and Jude;
Linus, Cletus, Clement, Sixtus,
Cornelius, Cyprian,
Lawrence, Chrysogonus,
John and Paul,
Cosmas and Damian)
and all your Saints;
we ask that through their merits and prayers,
in all things we may be defended
by your protecting help.
(Through Christ our Lord. Amen.)

PROPER FORMS OF THE COMMUNICANTES

On the Nativity of the Lord and throughout the Octave

**Celebrating the most sacred night (day)
on which blessed Mary the immaculate Virgin
brought forth the Savior for this world,
and in communion with those whose memory we venerate,
especially the glorious ever-Virgin Mary,
Mother of our God and Lord, Jesus Christ, †**

On the Epiphany of the Lord

**Celebrating the most sacred day
on which your Only Begotten Son,
eternal with you in your glory,
appeared in a human body, truly sharing our flesh,
and in communion with those whose memory we venerate,
especially the glorious ever-Virgin Mary,
Mother of our God and Lord, Jesus Christ, †**

From the Mass of the Easter Vigil until the Second Sunday of Easter

**Celebrating the most sacred night (day)
of the Resurrection of our Lord Jesus Christ in the flesh,
and in communion with those whose memory we venerate,
especially the glorious ever-Virgin Mary,
Mother of our God and Lord, Jesus Christ, †**

On the Ascension of the Lord

**Celebrating the most sacred day
on which your Only Begotten Son, our Lord,
placed at the right hand of your glory
our weak human nature,
which he had united to himself,
and in communion with those whose memory we venerate,
especially the glorious ever-Virgin Mary,
Mother of our God and Lord, Jesus Christ, †**

On Pentecost Sunday

**Celebrating the most sacred day of Pentecost,
on which the Holy Spirit
appeared to the Apostles in tongues of fire,
and in communion with those whose memory we venerate,
especially the glorious ever-Virgin Mary,
Mother of our God and Lord, Jesus Christ, †**

87. With hands extended, the Priest continues:

Therefore, Lord, we pray:
graciously accept this oblation of our service,
that of your whole family;
order our days in your peace,
and command that we be delivered from eternal damnation
and counted among the flock of those you have chosen.

He joins his hands.

(Through Christ our Lord. Amen.)

From the Mass of the Easter Vigil until the Second Sunday of Easter

Therefore, Lord, we pray:
graciously accept this oblation of our service,
that of your whole family,
which we make to you
also for those to whom you have been pleased to give
the new birth of water and the Holy Spirit,
granting them forgiveness of all their sins;
order our days in your peace,
and command that we be delivered from eternal damnation
and counted among the flock of those you have chosen.

He joins his hands.
(Through Christ our Lord. Amen.)

88. Holding his hands extended over the offerings, he says:

Be pleased, O God, we pray,
to bless, acknowledge,
and approve this offering in every respect;
make it spiritual and acceptable,
so that it may become for us
the Body and Blood of your most beloved Son,
our Lord Jesus Christ.

He joins his hands.

89.   In the formulas that follow, the words of the Lord should be pronounced clearly and distinctly, as the nature of these words requires.

On the day before he was to suffer,

He takes the bread
and, holding it slightly raised above the altar, continues:

he took bread in his holy and venerable hands,

He raises his eyes.

**and with eyes raised to heaven
to you, O God, his almighty Father,
giving you thanks, he said the blessing,
broke the bread
and gave it to his disciples, saying:**

He bows slightly.

TAKE THIS, ALL OF YOU, AND EAT OF IT,

FOR THIS IS MY BODY,

WHICH WILL BE GIVEN UP FOR YOU.

He shows the consecrated host to the people, places it again on the paten, and genuflects in adoration.

90.   After this, the Priest continues:

In a similar way, when supper was ended,

He takes the chalice
and, holding it slightly raised above the altar, continues:

**he took this precious chalice
in his holy and venerable hands,
and once more giving you thanks, he said the blessing
and gave the chalice to his disciples, saying:**

He bows slightly.

TAKE THIS, ALL OF YOU, AND DRINK FROM IT,

FOR THIS IS THE CHALICE OF MY BLOOD,

THE BLOOD OF THE NEW AND ETERNAL COVENANT,

WHICH WILL BE POURED OUT FOR YOU AND FOR MANY

FOR THE FORGIVENESS OF SINS.

DO THIS IN MEMORY OF ME.

He shows the chalice to the people, places it on the corporal, and genuflects in adoration.

91.   Then he says:

The mystery of faith.

And the people continue, acclaiming:

We proclaim your Death, O Lord,
and profess your Resurrection
until you come again.

Or:

When we eat this Bread and drink this Cup,
we proclaim your Death, O Lord,
until you come again.

Or:

Save us, Savior of the world,
for by your Cross and Resurrection
you have set us free.

92.   Then the Priest, with hands extended, says:

Therefore, O Lord,
as we celebrate the memorial of the blessed Passion,
the Resurrection from the dead,
and the glorious Ascension into heaven
of Christ, your Son, our Lord,
we, your servants and your holy people,
offer to your glorious majesty
from the gifts that you have given us,
this pure victim,
this holy victim,
this spotless victim,
the holy Bread of eternal life
and the Chalice of everlasting salvation.

93.   **Be pleased to look upon these offerings**
with a serene and kindly countenance,
and to accept them,
as once you were pleased to accept
the gifts of your servant Abel the just,
the sacrifice of Abraham, our father in faith,
and the offering of your high priest Melchizedek,
a holy sacrifice, a spotless victim.

94.　Bowing, with hands joined, he continues:

In humble prayer we ask you, almighty God:
command that these gifts be borne
by the hands of your holy Angel
to your altar on high
in the sight of your divine majesty,
so that all of us, who through this participation at the altar
receive the most holy Body and Blood of your Son,

He stands upright again and signs himself with the Sign of the Cross, saying:

may be filled with every grace and heavenly blessing.

He joins his hands.

(Through Christ our Lord. Amen.)

95.　Commemoration of the Dead

With hands extended, the Priest says:

Remember also, Lord, your servants N. **and** N.,
who have gone before us with the sign of faith
and rest in the sleep of peace.

He joins his hands and prays briefly for those who have died and for whom he intends to pray.

Then, with hands extended, he continues:

Grant them, O Lord, we pray,
and all who sleep in Christ,
a place of refreshment, light and peace.

He joins his hands.

(Through Christ our Lord. Amen.)

96. He strikes his breast with his right hand, saying:

To us, also, your servants, who, though sinners,

And, with hands extended, he continues:

hope in your abundant mercies,
graciously grant some share
and fellowship with your holy Apostles and Martyrs:
with John the Baptist, Stephen,
Matthias, Barnabas,
(Ignatius, Alexander,
Marcellinus, Peter,
Felicity, Perpetua,
Agatha, Lucy,
Agnes, Cecilia, Anastasia)
and all your Saints;
admit us, we beseech you,
into their company,
not weighing our merits,
but granting us your pardon,

He joins his hands.

through Christ our Lord.

97. And he continues:

Through whom
you continue to make all these good things, O Lord;
you sanctify them, fill them with life,
bless them, and bestow them upon us.

98. He takes the chalice and the paten with the host and, raising both, he says:

Through him, and with him, and in him,
O God, almighty Father,
in the unity of the Holy Spirit,
all glory and honor is yours,
for ever and ever.

The people acclaim:

Amen.

Then follows the Communion Rite, p. 000.

EUCHARISTIC PRAYER II

99.   Although it is provided with its own Preface, this Eucharistic Prayer may also be used with other Prefaces, especially those that present an overall view of the mystery of salvation, such as the Common Prefaces.

℣. **The Lord be with you.**
℟. **And with your spirit.**

℣. **Lift up your hearts.**
℟. **We lift them up to the Lord.**

℣. **Let us give thanks to the Lord our God.**
℟. **It is right and just.**

**It is truly right and just, our duty and our salvation,
always and everywhere to give you thanks, Father most holy,
through your beloved Son, Jesus Christ,
your Word through whom you made all things,
whom you sent as our Savior and Redeemer,
incarnate by the Holy Spirit and born of the Virgin.**

**Fulfilling your will and gaining for you a holy people,
he stretched out his hands as he endured his Passion,
so as to break the bonds of death and manifest the resurrection.**

**And so, with the Angels and all the Saints
we declare your glory,
as with one voice we acclaim:**

**Holy, Holy, Holy Lord God of hosts.
Heaven and earth are full of your glory.
Hosanna in the highest.
Blessed is he who comes in the name of the Lord.
Hosanna in the highest.**

100. The Priest, with hands extended, says:

**You are indeed Holy, O Lord,
the fount of all holiness.**

101. He joins his hands and, holding them extended over the offerings, says:

**Make holy, therefore, these gifts, we pray,
by sending down your Spirit upon them like the dewfall,**

He joins his hands
and makes the Sign of the Cross once over the bread and the chalice together, saying:

**so that they may become for us
the Body and ✠ Blood of our Lord Jesus Christ.**

He joins his hands.

102. In the formulas that follow, the words of the Lord should be pronounced clearly and distinctly, as the nature of these words requires.

**At the time he was betrayed
and entered willingly into his Passion,**

He takes the bread
and, holding it slightly raised above the altar, continues:

**he took bread and, giving thanks, broke it,
and gave it to his disciples, saying:**

He bows slightly.

TAKE THIS, ALL OF YOU, AND EAT OF IT,

FOR THIS IS MY BODY,

WHICH WILL BE GIVEN UP FOR YOU.

He shows the consecrated host to the people, places it again on the paten, and genuflects in adoration.

103. After this, he continues:

In a similar way, when supper was ended,

He takes the chalice
and, holding it slightly raised above the altar, continues:

**he took the chalice
and, once more giving thanks,
he gave it to his disciples, saying:**

He bows slightly.

TAKE THIS, ALL OF YOU, AND DRINK FROM IT,

FOR THIS IS THE CHALICE OF MY BLOOD,

THE BLOOD OF THE NEW AND ETERNAL COVENANT,

WHICH WILL BE POURED OUT FOR YOU AND FOR MANY

FOR THE FORGIVENESS OF SINS.

DO THIS IN MEMORY OF ME.

He shows the chalice to the people, places it on the corporal, and genuflects in adoration.

104.　Then he says:

The mystery of faith.

And the people continue, acclaiming:

We proclaim your Death, O Lord,
and profess your Resurrection
until you come again.

Or:

When we eat this Bread and drink this Cup,
we proclaim your Death, O Lord,
until you come again.

Or:

Save us, Savior of the world,
for by your Cross and Resurrection
you have set us free.

105. Then the Priest, with hands extended, says:

Therefore, as we celebrate
the memorial of his Death and Resurrection,
we offer you, Lord,
the Bread of life and the Chalice of salvation,
giving thanks that you have held us worthy
to be in your presence and minister to you.

Humbly we pray
that, partaking of the Body and Blood of Christ,
we may be gathered into one by the Holy Spirit.

Remember, Lord, your Church,
spread throughout the world,
and bring her to the fullness of charity,
together with N. our Pope and N. our Bishop*
and all the clergy.

---

* Mention may be made here of the Coadjutor Bishop, or Auxiliary Bishops, as noted in the *General Instruction of the Roman Missal*, no. 149.

In Masses for the Dead, the following may be added:

**Remember your servant N.,
whom you have called (today)
from this world to yourself.
Grant that he (she) who was united with your Son in a death like his,
may also be one with him in his Resurrection.**

**Remember also our brothers and sisters
who have fallen asleep in the hope of the resurrection,
and all who have died in your mercy:
welcome them into the light of your face.
Have mercy on us all, we pray,
that with the Blessed Virgin Mary, Mother of God,
with the blessed Apostles,
and all the Saints who have pleased you throughout the ages,
we may merit to be co-heirs to eternal life,
and may praise and glorify you**

He joins his hands.

through your Son, Jesus Christ.

106. He takes the chalice and the paten with the host and, raising both, he says:

**Through him, and with him, and in him,
O God, almighty Father,
in the unity of the Holy Spirit,
all glory and honor is yours,
for ever and ever.**

The people acclaim:

Amen.

Then follows the Communion Rite, p.**000**.

EUCHARISTIC PRAYER III

107. ℣. **The Lord be with you.**
℟. **And with your spirit.**

℣. **Lift up your hearts.**
℟. **We lift them up to the Lord.**

℣. **Let us give thanks to the Lord our God.**
℟. **It is right and just.**

Then follows the Preface to be used in accord with the rubrics, which concludes:

Holy, Holy, Holy Lord God of hosts.
Heaven and earth are full of your glory.
Hosanna in the highest.
Blessed is he who comes in the name of the Lord.
Hosanna in the highest.

108. The Priest, with hands extended, says:

You are indeed Holy, O Lord,
and all you have created
rightly gives you praise,
for through your Son our Lord Jesus Christ,
by the power and working of the Holy Spirit,
you give life to all things and make them holy,
and you never cease to gather a people to yourself,
so that from the rising of the sun to its setting
a pure sacrifice may be offered to your name.

109. He joins his hands and, holding them extended over the offerings, says:

Therefore, O Lord, we humbly implore you:
by the same Spirit graciously make holy
these gifts we have brought to you for consecration,

He joins his hands
and makes the Sign of the Cross once over the bread and chalice together, saying:

that they may become the Body and ✠ Blood
of your Son our Lord Jesus Christ,

He joins his hands.

at whose command we celebrate these mysteries.

110. In the formulas that follow, the words of the Lord should be pronounced clearly and distinctly, as the nature of these words requires.

For on the night he was betrayed

He takes the bread
and, holding it slightly raised above the altar, continues:

he himself took bread,
and, giving you thanks, he said the blessing,
broke the bread and gave it to his disciples, saying:

He bows slightly.

TAKE THIS, ALL OF YOU, AND EAT OF IT,

FOR THIS IS MY BODY,

WHICH WILL BE GIVEN UP FOR YOU.

He shows the consecrated host to the people, places it again on the paten, and genuflects in adoration.

111. After this, he continues:

In a similar way, when supper was ended,

He takes the chalice
and, holding it slightly raised above the altar, continues:

he took the chalice,
and, giving you thanks, he said the blessing,
and gave the chalice to his disciples, saying:

He bows slightly.

TAKE THIS, ALL OF YOU, AND DRINK FROM IT,

FOR THIS IS THE CHALICE OF MY BLOOD,

THE BLOOD OF THE NEW AND ETERNAL COVENANT,

WHICH WILL BE POURED OUT FOR YOU AND FOR MANY

FOR THE FORGIVENESS OF SINS.

DO THIS IN MEMORY OF ME.

He shows the chalice to the people, places it on the corporal, and genuflects in adoration.

112. Then he says:

The mystery of faith.

And the people continue, acclaiming:

**We proclaim your Death, O Lord,
and profess your Resurrection
until you come again.**

Or:

**When we eat this Bread and drink this Cup,
we proclaim your Death, O Lord,
until you come again.**

Or:

**Save us, Savior of the world,
for by your Cross and Resurrection
you have set us free.**

113. Then the Priest, with hands extended, says:

**Therefore, O Lord, as we celebrate the memorial
of the saving Passion of your Son,
his wondrous Resurrection
and Ascension into heaven,
and as we look forward to his second coming,
we offer you in thanksgiving
this holy and living sacrifice.**

**Look, we pray, upon the oblation of your Church
and, recognizing the sacrificial Victim by whose death
you willed to reconcile us to yourself,
grant that we, who are nourished
by the Body and Blood of your Son
and filled with his Holy Spirit,
may become one body, one spirit in Christ.**

**May he make of us
an eternal offering to you,
so that we may obtain an inheritance with your elect,
especially with the most Blessed Virgin Mary, Mother of God,
with your blessed Apostles and glorious Martyrs
(with Saint N.: the Saint of the day or Patron Saint)
and with all the Saints,
on whose constant intercession in your presence
we rely for unfailing help.**

May this Sacrifice of our reconciliation,
we pray, O Lord,
advance the peace and salvation of all the world.

Be pleased to confirm in faith and charity
your pilgrim Church on earth,
with your servant N. our Pope and N. our Bishop,*
the Order of Bishops, all the clergy,
and the entire people you have gained for your own.

Listen graciously to the prayers of this family,
whom you have summoned before you:
in your compassion, O merciful Father,
gather to yourself all your children
scattered throughout the world.

† To our departed brothers and sisters
and to all who were pleasing to you
at their passing from this life,
give kind admittance to your kingdom.
There we hope to enjoy for ever the fullness of your glory

He joins his hands.

through Christ our Lord,
through whom you bestow on the world all that is good. †

114. He takes the chalice and the paten with the host and, raising both, he says:

Through him, and with him, and in him,
O God, almighty Father,
in the unity of the Holy Spirit,
all glory and honor is yours,
for ever and ever.

The people acclaim:

Amen.

Then follows the Communion Rite, p.000.

---

    * Mention may be made here of the Coadjutor Bishop, or Auxiliary Bishops, as
noted in the *General Instruction of the Roman Missal*, no. 149.

115. When this Eucharistic Prayer is used in Masses for the Dead, the following may be said:

† **Remember your servant N.**
whom you have called (today)
from this world to yourself.
Grant that he (she) who was united with your Son in a death like his,
may also be one with him in his Resurrection,
when from the earth
he will raise up in the flesh those who have died,
and transform our lowly body
after the pattern of his own glorious body.
To our departed brothers and sisters, too,
and to all who were pleasing to you
at their passing from this life,
give kind admittance to your kingdom.
There we hope to enjoy for ever the fullness of your glory,
when you will wipe away every tear from our eyes.
For seeing you, our God, as you are,
we shall be like you for all the ages
and praise you without end,

He joins his hands.

through Christ our Lord,
through whom you bestow on the world all that is good. †

EUCHARISTIC PRAYER IV

116. It is not permitted to change the Preface of this Eucharistic Prayer because of the structure of the Prayer itself, which presents a summary of the history of salvation.

℣. **The Lord be with you.**
℟. **And with your spirit.**

℣. **Lift up your hearts.**
℟. **We lift them up to the Lord.**

℣. **Let us give thanks to the Lord our God.**
℟. **It is right and just.**

It is truly right to give you thanks,
truly just to give you glory, Father most holy,
for you are the one God living and true,
existing before all ages and abiding for all eternity,
dwelling in unapproachable light;
yet you, who alone are good, the source of life,
have made all that is,
so that you might fill your creatures with blessings
and bring joy to many of them by the glory of your light.

And so, in your presence are countless hosts of Angels,
who serve you day and night
and, gazing upon the glory of your face,
glorify you without ceasing.

With them we, too, confess your name in exultation,
giving voice to every creature under heaven,
as we acclaim:

Holy, Holy, Holy Lord God of hosts.
Heaven and earth are full of your glory.
Hosanna in the highest.
Blessed is he who comes in the name of the Lord.
Hosanna in the highest.

117. The Priest, with hands extended, says:

We give you praise, Father most holy,
for you are great
and you have fashioned all your works
in wisdom and in love.
You formed man in your own image
and entrusted the whole world to his care,
so that in serving you alone, the Creator,
he might have dominion over all creatures.
And when through disobedience he had lost your friendship,
you did not abandon him to the domain of death.
For you came in mercy to the aid of all,
so that those who seek might find you.
Time and again you offered them covenants
and through the prophets
taught them to look forward to salvation.

And you so loved the world, Father most holy,
that in the fullness of time
you sent your Only Begotten Son to be our Savior.
Made incarnate by the Holy Spirit
and born of the Virgin Mary,
he shared our human nature
in all things but sin.
To the poor he proclaimed the good news of salvation,
to prisoners, freedom,
and to the sorrowful of heart, joy.
To accomplish your plan,
he gave himself up to death,
and, rising from the dead,
he destroyed death and restored life.

And that we might live no longer for ourselves
but for him who died and rose again for us,
he sent the Holy Spirit from you, Father,
as the first fruits for those who believe,
so that, bringing to perfection his work in the world,
he might sanctify creation to the full.

118. He joins his hands and, holding them extended over the offerings, says:

Therefore, O Lord, we pray:
may this same Holy Spirit
graciously sanctify these offerings,

He joins his hands
and makes the Sign of the Cross once over the bread and chalice together, saying:

that they may become
the Body and ✠ Blood of our Lord Jesus Christ

He joins his hands.

for the celebration of this great mystery,
which he himself left us
as an eternal covenant.

119. In the formulas that follow, the words of the Lord should be pronounced clearly and distinctly, as the nature of these words requires.

For when the hour had come
for him to be glorified by you, Father most holy,
having loved his own who were in the world,
he loved them to the end:
and while they were at supper,

He takes the bread
and, holding it slightly raised above the altar, continues:

he took bread, blessed and broke it,
and gave it to his disciples, saying,

He bows slightly.

TAKE THIS, ALL OF YOU, AND EAT OF IT,

FOR THIS IS MY BODY,

WHICH WILL BE GIVEN UP FOR YOU.

He shows the consecrated host to the people, places it again on the paten, and genuflects in adoration.

120. After this, he continues:

In a similar way,

He takes the chalice
and, holding it slightly raised above the altar, continues:

**taking the chalice filled with the fruit of the vine,
he gave thanks,
and gave the chalice to his disciples, saying:**

He bows slightly.

TAKE THIS, ALL OF YOU, AND DRINK FROM IT,

FOR THIS IS THE CHALICE OF MY BLOOD,

THE BLOOD OF THE NEW AND ETERNAL COVENANT,

WHICH WILL BE POURED OUT FOR YOU AND FOR MANY

FOR THE FORGIVENESS OF SINS.

DO THIS IN MEMORY OF ME.

He shows the chalice to the people, places it on the corporal, and genuflects in adoration.

121. Then he says:

The mystery of faith.

And the people continue, acclaiming:

**We proclaim your Death, O Lord,
and profess your Resurrection
until you come again.**

Or:

**When we eat this Bread and drink this Cup,
we proclaim your Death, O Lord,
until you come again.**

Or:

**Save us, Savior of the world,
for by your Cross and Resurrection
you have set us free.**

122. Then, with hands extended, the Priest says:

Therefore, O Lord,
as we now celebrate the memorial of our redemption,
we remember Christ's Death
and his descent to the realm of the dead,
we proclaim his Resurrection
and his Ascension to your right hand,
and, as we await his coming in glory,
we offer you his Body and Blood,
the sacrifice acceptable to you
which brings salvation to the whole world.

Look, O Lord, upon the Sacrifice
which you yourself have provided for your Church,
and grant in your loving kindness
to all who partake of this one Bread and one Chalice
that, gathered into one body by the Holy Spirit,
they may truly become a living sacrifice in Christ
to the praise of your glory.

Therefore, Lord, remember now
all for whom we offer this sacrifice:
especially your servant, N. our Pope,
N. our Bishop, * **and the whole Order of Bishops,**
all the clergy,
those who take part in this offering,
those gathered here before you,
your entire people,
and all who seek you with a sincere heart.

Remember also
those who have died in the peace of your Christ
and all the dead,
whose faith you alone have known.

---

* Mention may be made here of the Coadjutor Bishop, or Auxiliary Bishops, as noted in the *General Instruction of the Roman Missal*, no. 149.

To all of us, your children,
grant, O merciful Father,
that we may enter into a heavenly inheritance
with the Blessed Virgin Mary, Mother of God,
and with your Apostles and Saints in your kingdom.
There, with the whole of creation,
freed from the corruption of sin and death,
may we glorify you through Christ our Lord,

He joins his hands.

through whom you bestow on the world all that is good.

123. He takes the chalice and the paten with the host and, raising both, he says:

Through him, and with him, and in him,
O God, almighty Father,
in the unity of the Holy Spirit,
all glory and honor is yours,
for ever and ever.

The people acclaim:

Amen.

Then follows the Communion Rite, p. 000.

The Communion Rite

124. After the chalice and paten have been set down, the Priest, with hands joined, says:

**At the Savior's command
and formed by divine teaching,
we dare to say:**

He extends his hands and, together with the people, continues:

**Our Father, who art in heaven,
hallowed be thy name;
thy kingdom come,
thy will be done
on earth as it is in heaven.
Give us this day our daily bread,
and forgive us our trespasses,
as we forgive those who trespass against us;
and lead us not into temptation,
but deliver us from evil.**

125. With hands extended, the Priest alone continues, saying:

**Deliver us, Lord, we pray, from every evil,
graciously grant peace in our days,
that, by the help of your mercy,
we may be always free from sin
and safe from all distress,
as we await the blessed hope
and the coming of our Savior, Jesus Christ.**

The Communion Rite

Since the Celebration of the Eucharist is the Paschal Banquet, it is desirable that in accordance with the Lord's command his Body and Blood should be received as spiritual food by those of the faithful who are properly disposed. This is the sense of the fraction and the other preparatory rites by which the faithful are led more immediately to Communion. (GIRM, no. 80)

The Lord's Prayer

In the Lord's Prayer a petition is made for daily bread, which for Christians means principally the Eucharistic Bread, and entreating also purification from sin, so that what is holy may in truth be given to the holy. The Priest pronounces the invitation to the prayer, and all the faithful say the prayer with him; then the Priest alone adds the embolism, which the people conclude by means of the doxology. The embolism, developing the last petition of the Lord's Prayer itself, asks for deliverance from the power of evil for the whole community of the faithful… (GIRM, no. 81)

He joins his hands.

The people conclude the prayer, acclaiming:

**For the kingdom,
the power and the glory are yours
now and for ever.**

126. Then the Priest, with hands extended, says aloud:

**Lord Jesus Christ,
who said to your Apostles:
Peace I leave you, my peace I give you;
look not on our sins,
but on the faith of your Church,
and graciously grant her peace and unity
in accordance with your will.**

He joins his hands.

Who live and reign for ever and ever.

The people reply:

Amen.

127. The Priest, turned towards the people, extending and then joining his hands, adds:

The peace of the Lord be with you always.

The people reply:

And with your spirit.

128. Then, if appropriate, the Deacon, or the Priest, adds:

Let us offer each other the sign of peace.

And all offer one another a sign, in keeping with local customs, that expresses peace, communion, and charity. The Priest gives the sign of peace to a Deacon or minister.

The Rite of Peace

There follows the Rite of Peace, by which the Church entreats peace and unity for herself and for the whole human family, and the faithful express to each other their ecclesial communion and mutual charity before communicating in the Sacrament.

As for the actual sign of peace to be given, the manner is to be established by the Conferences of Bishops in accordance with the culture and customs of the peoples. However, it is appropriate that each person offer the sign of peace only to those who are nearest and in a sober manner. (GIRM, no. 82)

129. Then he takes the host, breaks it over the paten, and places a small piece in the chalice, saying quietly:

May this mingling of the Body and Blood
of our Lord Jesus Christ
bring eternal life to us who receive it.

130. Meanwhile the following is sung or said:

Lamb of God, you take away the sins of the world,
     have mercy on us.
Lamb of God, you take away the sins of the world,
     have mercy on us.
Lamb of God, you take away the sins of the world,
     grant us peace.

The invocation may even be repeated several times if the fraction is prolonged. Only the final time, however, is grant us peace said.

131. Then the Priest, with hands joined, says quietly:

Lord Jesus Christ, Son of the living God,
who, by the will of the Father
and the work of the Holy Spirit,
through your Death gave life to the world,
free me by this, your most holy Body and Blood,
from all my sins and from every evil;
keep me always faithful to your commandments,
and never let me be parted from you.

Or:

May the receiving of your Body and Blood,
Lord Jesus Christ,
not bring me to judgment and condemnation,
but through your loving mercy
be for me protection in mind and body,
and a healing remedy.

The Fraction of the Bread

The Priest breaks the Eucharistic Bread, with the assistance, if the case requires, of the deacon or a concelebrant. The gesture of breaking bread done by Christ at the Last Supper, which in apostolic times gave the entire Eucharistic Action its name, signifies that the many faithful are made one body (*1 Cor* 10:17) by receiving Communion from the one Bread of Life which is Christ, who for the salvation of the world died and rose again. The fraction or breaking of bread is begun after the sign of peace and is carried out with proper reverence, and should not be unnecessarily prolonged or accorded exaggerated importance. This rite is reserved to the Priest and the deacon… (GIRM, no. 83)

132. The Priest genuflects, takes the host and, holding it slightly raised above the paten or above the chalice, while facing the people, says aloud:

Behold the Lamb of God,
behold him who takes away the sins of the world.
Blessed are those called to the supper of the Lamb.

And together with the people he adds once:

Lord, I am not worthy
that you should enter under my roof,
but only say the word
and my soul shall be healed.

133. The Priest, facing the altar, says quietly:

May the Body of Christ
keep me safe for eternal life.

And he reverently consumes the Body of Christ.

Then he takes the chalice and says quietly:

May the Blood of Christ
keep me safe for eternal life.

And he reverently consumes the Blood of Christ.

134. After this, he takes the paten or ciborium and approaches the communicants. The Priest raises a host slightly and shows it to each of the communicants, saying:

The Body of Christ.

The communicant replies:

Amen.

And receives Holy Communion.

If a Deacon also distributes Holy Communion, he does so in the same manner.

135. If any are present who are to receive Holy Communion under both kinds, the rite described in the proper place is to be followed.

Communion

The Priest prepares himself by a prayer, said quietly, so that he may fruitfully receive the Body and Blood of Christ. The faithful do the same, praying silently.

Then the Priest shows the faithful the Eucharistic Bread, holding it over the paten or over the chalice, and invites them to the banquet of Christ; and along with the faithful, he then makes an act of humility, using the prescribed words from the Gospels. (GIRM, no. 84)

136. While the Priest is receiving the Body of Christ, the Communion Chant begins.

137. When the distribution of Communion is over, the Priest or a Deacon or an acolyte purifies the paten over the chalice and also the chalice itself.

While he carries out the purification, the Priest says quietly:

What has passed our lips as food, O Lord,
may we possess in purity of heart,
that what has been given to us in time
may be our healing for eternity.

138. Then the Priest may return to the chair. If appropriate, a sacred silence may be observed for a while, or a psalm or other canticle of praise or a hymn may be sung.

139. Then, standing at the altar or at the chair and facing the people, with hands joined, the Priest says:

Let us pray.

All pray in silence with the Priest for a while, unless silence has just been observed. Then the Priest, with hands extended, says the Prayer after Communion, at the end of which the people acclaim:

Amen.

The Communion Chant

While the Priest is receiving the Sacrament, the Communion chant is begun, its purpose being to express the spiritual union of the communicants by means of the unity of their voices, to show gladness of heart, and to bring out more clearly the "communitarian" character of the procession to receive the Eucharist. The singing is prolonged for as long as the Sacrament is being administered to the faithful (Cf. Sacred Congregation for the Sacraments and Divine Worship, Instruction *Inestimabile donum*, 3 April 1980, no. 17: *Acta Apostolicæ Sedis* 72 (1980), p. 338). However, if there is to be a hymn after Communion, the Communion chant should be ended in a timely manner.

Care should be taken that singers, too, can receive Communion with ease. (GIRM, no. 86)

For singing at Communion, it is possible to use the antiphon from the *Graduale Romanum*, with or without the Psalm, or the antiphon with Psalm from the *Graduale Simplex*, or some other suitable liturgical chant approved by the Conference of Bishops. This is sung either by the choir alone or by the choir or a cantor with the people.

However, if there is no singing, the antiphon given in the Missal may be recited either by the faithful, or by some of them, or by a reader; otherwise, it is recited by the Priest himself after he has received Communion and before he distributes Communion to the faithful. (GIRM, no. 87)

The Concluding Rites

140. If they are necessary, any brief announcements to the people follow here.

141. Then the dismissal takes place. The Priest, facing the people and extending his hands, says:

The Lord be with you.

The people reply:

And with your spirit.

The Priest blesses the people, saying:

**May almighty God bless you,
the Father, and the Son, ✠ and the Holy Spirit.**

The people reply:

Amen.

---

142. On certain days or occasions, this formula of blessing is preceded, in accordance with the rubrics, by another more solemn formula of blessing or by a prayer over the people (cf. pp. **000ff.**).

---

143. In a Pontifical Mass, the celebrant receives the miter and, extending his hands, says:

The Lord be with you.

All reply:

And with your spirit.

THE CONCLUDING RITES

90.   To the Concluding Rites belong the following:

a) brief announcements, should they be necessary;

b) the Priest's greeting and blessing, which on certain days and occasions is expanded and expressed by the Prayer over the People or another more solemn formula;

c) the dismissal of the people by the deacon or the Priest, so that each may go back to doing good works, praising and blessing God;

d) the kissing of the altar by the Priest and the deacon, followed by a profound bow to the altar by the Priest, the deacon, and the other ministers. (GIRM, no. 90)

The celebrant says:
Blessed be the name of the Lord.

All reply:
Now and for ever.

The celebrant says:
Our help is in the name of the Lord.

All reply:
Who made heaven and earth.

Then the celebrant receives the pastoral staff, if he uses it, and says:
May almighty God bless you,

making the Sign of the Cross over the people three times, he adds:
the Father, ✠ and the Son, ✠ and the Holy ✠ Spirit.

All:
Amen.

144. Then the Deacon, or the Priest himself, with hands joined and facing the people, says:
Go forth, the Mass is ended.

Or:
Go and announce the Gospel of the Lord.

Or:
Go in peace, glorifying the Lord by your life.

Or:
Go in peace.

The people reply:
Thanks be to God.

145. Then the Priest venerates the altar as usual with a kiss, as at the beginning. After making a profound bow with the ministers, he withdraws.

146. If any liturgical action follows immediately, the rites of dismissal are omitted.

Notes

Notes

ADVENT

Advent has a twofold character, for it is a time of preparation for the Solemnities of Christmas, in which the First Coming of the Son of God to humanity is remembered, and likewise a time when, by remembrance of this, minds and hearts are led to look forward to Christ's Second Coming at the end of time. For these two reasons, Advent is a period of devout and expectant delight. (*Universal Norms on the Liturgical Year and the Calendar* [UNLYC], no. 39)

FIRST SUNDAY OF ADVENT

Entrance Antiphon

Cf. Ps 25 (24): 1–3

To you, I lift up my soul, O my God.
In you, I have trusted; let me not be put to shame.
Nor let my enemies exult over me;
and let none who hope in you be put to shame.

The Gloria in excelsis (Glory to God in the highest) is not said.

Collect

Grant your faithful, we pray, almighty God,
the resolve to run forth to meet your Christ
with righteous deeds at his coming,
so that, gathered at his right hand,
they may be worthy to possess the heavenly kingdom.
Through our Lord Jesus Christ, your Son,
who lives and reigns with you in the unity of the Holy Spirit,
one God, for ever and ever.

The Creed is said.

Prayer over the Offerings

Accept, we pray, O Lord, these offerings we make,
gathered from among your gifts to us,
and may what you grant us to celebrate devoutly here below
gain for us the prize of eternal redemption.
Through Christ our Lord.

Preface I of Advent, p. 000.

Communion Antiphon   Ps 85 (84):13

The Lord will bestow his bounty, and our earth shall yield its increase.

Prayer after Communion

May these mysteries, O Lord,
in which we have participated,
profit us, we pray,
for even now, as we walk amid passing things,
you teach us by them to love the things of heaven
and hold fast to what endures.
Through Christ our Lord.

A formula of Solemn Blessing, p.000, may be used.

SECOND SUNDAY OF ADVENT

Entrance Antiphon
Cf. Is 30:19, 30

O people of Sion, behold,
the Lord will come to save the nations,
and the Lord will make the glory of his voice heard
in the joy of your heart.

The Gloria in excelsis (Glory to God in the highest) is not said.

Collect

**Almighty and merciful God,
may no earthly undertaking hinder those
who set out in haste to meet your Son,
but may our learning of heavenly wisdom
gain us admittance to his company.
Who lives and reigns with you in the unity of the Holy Spirit,
one God, for ever and ever.**

The Creed is said.

Prayer over the Offerings

**Be pleased, O Lord, with our humble prayers and offerings,
and, since we have no merits to plead our cause,
come, we pray, to our rescue
with the protection of your mercy.
Through Christ our Lord.**

Preface I of Advent, p. **000**.

Communion Antiphon
Bar 5:5; 4:36

**Jerusalem, arise and stand upon the heights,
and behold the joy which comes to you from God.**

Prayer after Communion

**Replenished by the food of spiritual nourishment,
we humbly beseech you, O Lord,
that, through our partaking in this mystery,
you may teach us to judge wisely the things of earth
and hold firm to the things of heaven.
Through Christ our Lord.**

A formula of Solemn Blessing, p. **000**, may be used.

THIRD SUNDAY OF ADVENT

In this Mass the color violet or rose is used.

Entrance Antiphon   Phil 4: 4–5

Rejoice in the Lord always; again I say, rejoice.
Indeed, the Lord is near.

The Gloria in excelsis (Glory to God in the highest) is not said.

Collect

O God, who see how your people
faithfully await the feast of the Lord's Nativity,
enable us, we pray,
to attain the joys of so great a salvation
and to celebrate them always
with solemn worship and glad rejoicing.
Through our Lord Jesus Christ, your Son,
who lives and reigns with you in the unity of the Holy Spirit,
one God, for ever and ever.

The Creed is said.

Prayer over the Offerings

May the sacrifice of our worship, Lord, we pray,
be offered to you unceasingly,
to complete what was begun in sacred mystery
and powerfully accomplish for us your saving work.
Through Christ our Lord.

Preface I or II of Advent, pp. 000–000.

Communion Antiphon   Cf. Is 35: 4

Say to the faint of heart: Be strong and do not fear.
Behold, our God will come, and he will save us.

Prayer after Communion

We implore your mercy, Lord,
that this divine sustenance may cleanse us of our faults
and prepare us for the coming feasts.
Through Christ our Lord.

A formula of Solemn Blessing, p. 000, may be used.

FOURTH SUNDAY OF ADVENT

Entrance Antiphon

Cf. Is 45:8

Drop down dew from above, you heavens,
and let the clouds rain down the Just One;
let the earth be opened and bring forth a Savior.

The Gloria in excelsis (Glory to God in the highest) is not said.

Collect

Pour forth, we beseech you, O Lord,
your grace into our hearts,
that we, to whom the Incarnation of Christ your Son
was made known by the message of an Angel,
may by his Passion and Cross
be brought to the glory of his Resurrection.
Who lives and reigns with you in the unity of the Holy Spirit,
one God, for ever and ever.

The Creed is said.

Prayer over the Offerings

May the Holy Spirit, O Lord,
sanctify these gifts laid upon your altar,
just as he filled with his power the womb of the Blessed Virgin Mary.
Through Christ our Lord.

Preface II of Advent, p. **000**.

Communion Antiphon

Is 7:14

Behold, a Virgin shall conceive and bear a son;
and his name will be called Emmanuel.

Prayer after Communion

Having received this pledge of eternal redemption,
we pray, almighty God,
that, as the feast day of our salvation draws ever nearer,
so we may press forward all the more eagerly
to the worthy celebration of the mystery of your Son's Nativity.
Who lives and reigns for ever and ever.

A formula of Solemn Blessing, p. **000**, may be used.

CHRISTMAS TIME

25 December

THE NATIVITY OF THE LORD

Solemnity

After the annual celebration of the Paschal Mystery, the Church has no more ancient custom than celebrating the memorial of the Nativity of the Lord and of his first manifestations, and this takes place in Christmas Time. (UNLYC, no. 32)

At the Vigil Mass

This Mass is used on the evening of December 24, either before or after First Vespers (Evening Prayer I) of the Nativity.

Entrance Antiphon

Cf. Ex 16:6–7

**Today you will know that the Lord will come, and he will save us,
and in the morning you will see his glory.**

The Gloria in excelsis (Glory to God in the highest) is said.

Collect

**O God, who gladden us year by year
as we wait in hope for our redemption,
grant that, just as we joyfully welcome
your Only Begotten Son as our Redeemer,
we may also merit to face him confidently
when he comes again as our Judge.
Who lives and reigns with you in the unity of the Holy Spirit,
one God, for ever and ever.**

The Creed is said. All kneel at the words **and by the Holy Spirit was incarnate**.

Prayer over the Offerings

**As we look forward, O Lord,
to the coming festivities,
may we serve you all the more eagerly
for knowing that in them
you make manifest the beginnings of our redemption.
Through Christ our Lord.**

Preface I, II or III of the Nativity of the Lord, pp. 000–000.

When the Roman Canon is used, the proper form of the **Communicantes (In communion with those)** is said.

Communion Antiphon   Cf. Is 40:5

The glory of the Lord will be revealed,
and all flesh will see the salvation of our God.

Prayer after Communion

Grant, O Lord, we pray,
that we may draw new vigor
from celebrating the Nativity of your Only Begotten Son,
by whose heavenly mystery we receive both food and drink.
Who lives and reigns for ever and ever.

A formula of Solemn Blessing, p. 000, may be used.

At the Mass during the Night

On the Nativity of the Lord all Priests may celebrate or concelebrate three Masses, provided the Masses are celebrated at their proper times.

Entrance Antiphon   Ps 2:7

The Lord said to me: You are my Son.
It is I who have begotten you this day.

Or:

Let us all rejoice in the Lord, for our Savior has been born in the world.
Today true peace has come down to us from heaven.

The Gloria in excelsis (Glory to God in the highest) is said.

Collect

O God, who have made this most sacred night
radiant with the splendor of the true light,
grant, we pray, that we, who have known the mysteries of his light on earth,
may also delight in his gladness in heaven.
Who lives and reigns with you in the unity of the Holy Spirit,
one God, for ever and ever.

The Creed is said. All kneel at the words and by the Holy Spirit was incarnate.

Prayer over the Offerings

May the oblation of this day's feast
be pleasing to you, O Lord, we pray,
that through this most holy exchange
we may be found in the likeness of Christ,
in whom our nature is united to you.
Who lives and reigns for ever and ever.

Preface I, II or III of the Nativity of the Lord, pp. **000–000**.

When the Roman Canon is used, the proper form of the Communicantes (In communion with those) is said.

Communion Antiphon   Jn 1:14

The Word became flesh, and we have seen his glory.

Prayer after Communion

Grant us, we pray, O Lord our God,
that we, who are gladdened by participation
in the feast of our Redeemer's Nativity,
may through an honorable way of life become worthy of union with him.
Who lives and reigns for ever and ever.

A formula of Solemn Blessing, p. 000, may be used.

At the Mass at Dawn

Entrance Antiphon
Cf. Is 9: 1, 5; Lk 1: 33

Today a light will shine upon us, for the Lord is born for us;
and he will be called Wondrous God,
Prince of peace, Father of future ages:
and his reign will be without end.

The Gloria in excelsis (Glory to God in the highest) is said.

Collect

Grant, we pray, almighty God,
that, as we are bathed in the new radiance of your incarnate Word,
the light of faith, which illumines our minds,
may also shine through in our deeds.
Through our Lord Jesus Christ, your Son,
who lives and reigns with you in the unity of the Holy Spirit,
one God, for ever and ever.

The Creed is said. All kneel at the words and by the Holy Spirit was incarnate.

Prayer over the Offerings

May our offerings be worthy, we pray, O Lord,
of the mysteries of the Nativity this day,
that, just as Christ was born a man and also shone forth as God,
so these earthly gifts may confer on us what is divine.
Through Christ our Lord.

Preface I, II or III of the Nativity of the Lord, pp. 000–000.

When the Roman Canon is used, the proper form of the Communicantes (In communion with those) is said.

Communion Antiphon   Cf. Zec 9 : 9

Rejoice, O Daughter Sion; lift up praise, Daughter Jerusalem:
Behold, your King will come, the Holy One and Savior of the world.

Prayer after Communion

Grant us, Lord, as we honor with joyful devotion
the Nativity of your Son,
that we may come to know with fullness of faith
the hidden depths of this mystery
and to love them ever more and more.
Through Christ our Lord.

A formula of Solemn Blessing, p. **000**, may be used.

At the Mass during the Day

Entrance Antiphon

Cf. Is 9:5

A child is born for us, and a son is given to us;
his scepter of power rests upon his shoulder,
and his name will be called Messenger of great counsel.

The Gloria in excelsis (Glory to God in the highest) is said.

Collect

O God, who wonderfully created the dignity of human nature
and still more wonderfully restored it,
grant, we pray,
that we may share in the divinity of Christ,
who humbled himself to share in our humanity.
Who lives and reigns with you in the unity of the Holy Spirit,
one God, for ever and ever.

The Creed is said. All kneel at the words and by the Holy Spirit was incarnate.

Prayer over the Offerings

Make acceptable, O Lord, our oblation on this solemn day,
when you manifested the reconciliation
that makes us wholly pleasing in your sight
and inaugurated for us the fullness of divine worship.
Through Christ our Lord.

Preface I, II or III of the Nativity of the Lord, pp. 000–000.

When the Roman Canon is used, the proper form of the Communicantes (In communion with those) is said.

Communion Antiphon

Cf. Ps 98 (97):3

All the ends of the earth have seen the salvation of our God.

Prayer after Communion

Grant, O merciful God,
that, just as the Savior of the world, born this day,
is the author of divine generation for us,
so he may be the giver even of immortality.
Who lives and reigns for ever and ever.

A formula of Solemn Blessing, p. 000, may be used.

The Sunday within the Octave of the Nativity of the Lord [Christmas], or, if there is no Sunday, December 30.

THE HOLY FAMILY OF JESUS, MARY AND JOSEPH
Feast

Entrance Antiphon   Lk 2:16

The shepherds went in haste,
and found Mary and Joseph and the Infant lying in a manger.

The Gloria in excelsis (Glory to God in the highest) is said.

Collect

O God, who were pleased to give us
the shining example of the Holy Family,
graciously grant that we may imitate them
in practicing the virtues of family life and in the bonds of charity,
and so, in the joy of your house,
delight one day in eternal rewards.
Through our Lord Jesus Christ, your Son,
who lives and reigns with you in the unity of the Holy Spirit,
one God, for ever and ever.

When this Feast is celebrated on Sunday, the Creed is said.

Prayer over the Offerings

We offer you, Lord, the sacrifice of conciliation,
humbly asking that,
through the intercession of the Virgin Mother of God and Saint Joseph,
you may establish our families firmly in your grace and your peace.
Through Christ our Lord.

Preface I, II or III of the Nativity of the Lord, pp. 000–000.

When the Roman Canon is used, the proper form of the Communicantes (In communion with those) is said.

Communion Antiphon   Bar 3:38
Our God has appeared on the earth, and lived among us.

Prayer after Communion
Bring those you refresh with this heavenly Sacrament,
most merciful Father,
to imitate constantly the example of the Holy Family,
so that, after the trials of this world,
we may share their company for ever.
Through Christ our Lord.

January 1

The Octave Day of the Nativity of the Lord [Christmas]

SOLEMNITY OF MARY,
THE HOLY MOTHER OF GOD

Entrance Antiphon

Hail, Holy Mother, who gave birth to the King,
who rules heaven and earth for ever.

Or: Cf. Is 9:1, 5; Lk 1:33

Today a light will shine upon us, for the Lord is born for us;
and he will be called Wondrous God,
Prince of peace, Father of future ages:
and his reign will be without end.

The Gloria in excelsis (Glory to God in the highest) is said.

Collect

O God, who through the fruitful virginity of Blessed Mary
bestowed on the human race
the grace of eternal salvation,
grant, we pray,
that we may experience the intercession of her,
through whom we were found worthy
to receive the author of life,
our Lord Jesus Christ, your Son.
Who lives and reigns with you in the unity of the Holy Spirit,
one God, for ever and ever.

The Creed is said.

Prayer over the Offerings

O God, who in your kindness begin all good things
and bring them to fulfillment,
grant to us, who find joy in the Solemnity of the holy Mother of God,
that, just as we glory in the beginnings of your grace,
so one day we may rejoice in its completion.
Through Christ our Lord.

Preface I of the Blessed Virgin Mary (on the Solemnity of the Motherhood), pp. 000–000.

When the Roman Canon is used, the proper form of the **Communicantes** (In communion with those) is said.

Communion Antiphon   Heb 13:8

Jesus Christ is the same yesterday, today, and for ever.

Prayer after Communion

**We have received this heavenly Sacrament with joy, O Lord:
grant, we pray,
that it may lead us to eternal life,
for we rejoice to proclaim the blessed ever-Virgin Mary
Mother of your Son and Mother of the Church.
Through Christ our Lord.**

A formula of Solemn Blessing, p.000, may be used.

On the days following, when the Mass of the weekday is to be said, the texts given below are used, p.000.

SECOND SUNDAY AFTER THE NATIVITY [CHRISTMAS]

Entrance Antiphon   Wis 18:14–15

**When a profound silence covered all things
and night was in the middle of its course,
your all-powerful Word, O Lord, bounded from heaven's royal throne.**

The Gloria in excelsis (Glory to God in the highest) is said.

Collect

**Almighty ever-living God,
splendor of faithful souls,
graciously be pleased to fill the world with your glory,
and show yourself to all peoples by the radiance of your light.
Through our Lord Jesus Christ, your Son,
who lives and reigns with you in the unity of the Holy Spirit,
one God, for ever and ever.**

The Creed is said.

Prayer over the Offerings

**Sanctify, O Lord, the offerings we make
on the Nativity of your Only Begotten Son,
for by it you show us the way of truth
and promise the life of the heavenly Kingdom.
Through Christ our Lord.**

Preface I, II or III of the Nativity of the Lord, pp. 000–000.

Communion Antiphon   Cf. Jn 1:12

**To all who would accept him,
he gave the power to become children of God.**

Prayer after Communion

**Lord our God, we humbly ask you,
that, through the working of this mystery,
our offenses may be cleansed
and our just desires fulfilled.
Through Christ our Lord.**

A formula of Solemn Blessing, p. 000, may be used.

January 6

THE EPIPHANY OF THE LORD

Solemnity

Where the Solemnity of the Epiphany is not to be observed as a Holy Day of Obligation, it is assigned to the Sunday occurring between January 2 and 8 as its proper day.

At the Vigil Mass

This Mass is used on the evening of the day before the Solemnity, either before or after First Vespers (Evening Prayer I) of the Epiphany.

Entrance Antiphon   Cf. Bar 5:5

**Arise, Jerusalem, and look to the East
and see your children gathered from the rising to the setting of the sun.**

The Gloria in excelsis (Glory to God in the highest) is said.

Collect

**May the splendor of your majesty, O Lord, we pray,
shed its light upon our hearts,
that we may pass through the shadows of this world
and reach the brightness of our eternal home.
Through our Lord Jesus Christ, your Son,
who lives and reigns with you in the unity of the Holy Spirit,
one God, for ever and ever.**

The Creed is said.

Prayer over the Offerings

**Accept we pray, O Lord, our offerings,
in honor of the appearing of your Only Begotten Son
and the first fruits of the nations,
that to you praise may be rendered
and eternal salvation be ours.
Through Christ our Lord.**

Preface of the Epiphany of the Lord, pp. 000–000.

Communion Antiphon   Cf. Rev 21:23

**The brightness of God illumined the holy city Jerusalem,
and the nations will walk by its light.**

Prayer after Communion

**Renewed by sacred nourishment,
we implore your mercy, O Lord,
that the star of your justice
may shine always bright in our minds
and that our true treasure may ever consist in our confession of you.
Through Christ our Lord.**

A formula of Solemn Blessing, p. **000**, may be used.

At the Mass during the Day

Entrance Antiphon   Cf. Mal 3:1; 1 Chr 29:12
Behold, the Lord, the Mighty One, has come;
and kingship is in his grasp, and power and dominion.

The Gloria in excelsis (Glory to God in the highest) is said.

Collect
O God, who on this day
revealed your Only Begotten Son to the nations
by the guidance of a star,
grant in your mercy, that we, who know you already by faith,
may be brought to behold the beauty of your sublime glory.
Through our Lord Jesus Christ, your Son,
who lives and reigns with you in the unity of the Holy Spirit,
one God, for ever and ever.

Where it is the practice, if appropriate, the moveable Feasts of the current year may be proclaimed after the Gospel, according to the formula given below, pp. 0000–0000.

The Creed is said.

Prayer over the Offerings
Look with favor, Lord, we pray,
on these gifts of your Church,
in which are offered now not gold or frankincense or myrrh,
but he who by them is proclaimed,
sacrificed and received, Jesus Christ.
Who lives and reigns for ever and ever.

Preface of the Epiphany of the Lord, pp. 000–000.

Communion Antiphon   Cf. Mt 2:2

We have seen his star in the East,
and have come with gifts to adore the Lord.

Prayer after Communion

Go before us with heavenly light, O Lord,
always and everywhere,
that we may perceive with clear sight
and revere with true affection
the mystery in which you have willed us to participate.
Through Christ our Lord.

A formula of Solemn Blessing, p. 000, may be used.

Sunday after the Epiphany of the Lord

THE BAPTISM OF THE LORD

Feast

Where the Solemnity of the Epiphany is transferred to Sunday, if this Sunday occurs on January 7 or 8, the Feast of the Baptism of the Lord is celebrated on the following Monday.

Entrance Antiphon   Cf. Mt 3:16–17

After the Lord was baptized, the heavens were opened,
and the Spirit descended upon him like a dove,
and the voice of the Father thundered:
This is my beloved Son, with whom I am well pleased.

The Gloria in excelsis (Glory to God in the highest) is said.

Collect

Almighty ever-living God,
who, when Christ had been baptized in the River Jordan
and as the Holy Spirit descended upon him,
solemnly declared him your beloved Son,
grant that your children by adoption,
reborn of water and the Holy Spirit,
may always be well pleasing to you.
Through our Lord Jesus Christ, your Son,
who lives and reigns with you in the unity of the Holy Spirit,
one God, for ever and ever.

Or:

O God, whose Only Begotten Son
has appeared in our very flesh,
grant, we pray, that we may be inwardly transformed
through him whom we recognize as outwardly like ourselves.
Who lives and reigns with you in the unity of the Holy Spirit,
one God, for ever and ever.

The Creed is said.

Prayer over the Offerings

Accept, O Lord, the offerings
we have brought to honor the revealing of your beloved Son,
so that the oblation of your faithful
may be transformed into the sacrifice of him
who willed in his compassion
to wash away the sins of the world.
Who lives and reigns for ever and ever.

Preface: The Baptism of the Lord, p. 000.

Communion Antiphon   Jn 1:32, 34

Behold the One of whom John said:
I have seen and testified that this is the Son of God.

Prayer after Communion

Nourished with these sacred gifts,
we humbly entreat your mercy, O Lord,
that, faithfully listening to your Only Begotten Son,
we may be your children in name and in truth.
Through Christ our Lord.

Ordinary Time lasts from the Monday after this Sunday to the Tuesday before Lent. For Masses both on Sundays and on weekdays, the texts given below, pp. 000 ff., are used.

LENT

Lent is ordered to preparing for the celebration of Easter, since the Lenten liturgy prepares for celebration of the Paschal mystery both catechumens, by the various stages of Christian Initiation, and the faithful, who recall their own Baptism and do penance (Cf. Second Vatican Council, Constitution on the Sacred Liturgy *Sacrosanctum Concilium*, nos. 109). (UNLYC, no. 27)

FIRST SUNDAY OF LENT

On this Sunday is celebrated the rite of "election" or "enrollment of names" for the catechumens who are to be admitted to the Sacraments of Christian Initiation at the Easter Vigil, using the proper prayers and intercessions as given below, pp. **000–000**.

Entrance Antiphon   Cf. Ps 91 (90):15–16

When he calls on me, I will answer him;
I will deliver him and give him glory,
I will grant him length of days.

The Gloria in excelsis (Glory to God in the highest) is not said.

Collect

Grant, almighty God,
through the yearly observances of holy Lent,
that we may grow in understanding
of the riches hidden in Christ
and by worthy conduct pursue their effects.
Through our Lord Jesus Christ, your Son,
who lives and reigns with you in the unity of the Holy Spirit,
one God, for ever and ever.

The Creed is said.

Prayer over the Offerings

Give us the right dispositions, O Lord, we pray,
to make these offerings,
for with them we celebrate the beginning
of this venerable and sacred time.
Through Christ our Lord.

Preface: The Temptation of the Lord, p. **000**.

Communion Antiphon   Mt 4:4

One does not live by bread alone,
but by every word that comes forth from the mouth of God.

Or: Cf. Ps 91 (90): 4

The Lord will conceal you with his pinions,
and under his wings you will trust.

Prayer after Communion

Renewed now with heavenly bread,
by which faith is nourished, hope increased,
and charity strengthened,
we pray, O Lord,
that we may learn to hunger for Christ,
the true and living Bread,
and strive to live by every word
which proceeds from your mouth.
Through Christ our Lord.

Prayer over the People

May bountiful blessing, O Lord, we pray,
come down upon your people,
that hope may grow in tribulation,
virtue be strengthened in temptation,
and eternal redemption be assured.
Through Christ our Lord.

SECOND SUNDAY OF LENT

Entrance Antiphon
Cf. Ps 27 (26): 8–9

Of you my heart has spoken, Seek his face.
It is your face, O Lord, that I seek;
hide not your face from me.

Or:
Cf. Ps 25 (24): 6, 2, 22

Remember your compassion, O Lord,
and your merciful love, for they are from of old.
Let not our enemies exult over us.
Redeem us, O God of Israel, from all our distress.

The Gloria in excelsis (Glory to God in the highest) is not said.

Collect

O God, who have commanded us
to listen to your beloved Son,
be pleased, we pray,
to nourish us inwardly by your word,
that, with spiritual sight made pure,
we may rejoice to behold your glory.
Through our Lord Jesus Christ, your Son,
who lives and reigns with you in the unity of the Holy Spirit,
one God, for ever and ever.

The Creed is said.

Prayer over the Offerings

May this sacrifice, O Lord, we pray,
cleanse us of our faults
and sanctify your faithful in body and mind
for the celebration of the paschal festivities.
Through Christ our Lord.

Preface: The Transfiguration of the Lord, p. 000.

Communion Antiphon   Mt 17:5

This is my beloved Son, with whom I am well pleased;
listen to him.

Prayer after Communion

As we receive these glorious mysteries,
we make thanksgiving to you, O Lord,
for allowing us while still on earth
to be partakers even now of the things of heaven.
Through Christ our Lord.

Prayer over the People

Bless your faithful, we pray, O Lord,
with a blessing that endures for ever,
and keep them faithful
to the Gospel of your Only Begotten Son,
so that they may always desire and at last attain
that glory whose beauty he showed in his own Body,
to the amazement of his Apostles.
Through Christ our Lord.

THIRD SUNDAY OF LENT

On this Sunday is celebrated the first scrutiny in preparation for the Baptism of the catechumens who are to be admitted to the Sacraments of Christian Initiation at the Easter Vigil, using the proper prayers and intercessions as given below, pp. **000–000**.

Entrance Antiphon
Cf. Ps 25 (24): 15–16

My eyes are always on the Lord,
for he rescues my feet from the snare.
Turn to me and have mercy on me,
for I am alone and poor.

Or:
Cf. Ez 36: 23–26

When I prove my holiness among you,
I will gather you from all the foreign lands;
and I will pour clean water upon you
and cleanse you from all your impurities,
and I will give you a new spirit, says the Lord.

The Gloria in excelsis (Glory to God in the highest) is not said.

Collect

O God, author of every mercy and of all goodness,
who in fasting, prayer and almsgiving
have shown us a remedy for sin,
look graciously on this confession of our lowliness,
that we, who are bowed down by our conscience,
may always be lifted up by your mercy.
Through our Lord Jesus Christ, your Son,
who lives and reigns with you in the unity of the Holy Spirit,
one God, for ever and ever.

The Creed is said.

Prayer over the Offerings

Be pleased, O Lord, with these sacrificial offerings,
and grant that we who beseech pardon for our own sins,
may take care to forgive our neighbor.
Through Christ our Lord.

When the Gospel of the Samaritan Woman is not read, Preface I or II of Lent, pp. **000–000**, is used.

Preface: The Samaritan Woman, p. **000**.

Communion Antiphon

When the Gospel of the Samaritan Woman is read: Jn 4:13–14

**For anyone who drinks it, says the Lord,
the water I shall give will become in him
a spring welling up to eternal life.**

When another Gospel is read: Cf. Ps 84 (83):4–5

**The sparrow finds a home,
and the swallow a nest for her young:
by your altars, O Lord of hosts, my King and my God.
Blessed are they who dwell in your house,
for ever singing your praise.**

Prayer after Communion

**As we receive the pledge
of things yet hidden in heaven
and are nourished while still on earth
with the Bread that comes from on high,
we humbly entreat you, O Lord,
that what is being brought about in us in mystery
may come to true completion.
Through Christ our Lord.**

Prayer over the People

**Direct, O Lord, we pray, the hearts of your faithful,
and in your kindness grant your servants this grace:
that, abiding in the love of you and their neighbor,
they may fulfill the whole of your commands.
Through Christ our Lord.**

FOURTH SUNDAY OF LENT

In this Mass, the color violet or rose is used. Instrumental music is permitted, and the altar may be decorated with flowers.

On this Sunday is celebrated the second scrutiny in preparation for the Baptism of the catechumens who are to be admitted to the Sacraments of Christian Initiation at the Easter Vigil, using the proper prayers and intercessions as given below, pp. **000–000**.

Entrance Antiphon   Cf. Is 66:10–11

Rejoice, Jerusalem, and all who love her.
Be joyful, all who were in mourning;
exult and be satisfied at her consoling breast.

The Gloria in excelsis (Glory to God in the highest) is not said.

Collect

O God, who through your Word
reconcile the human race to yourself in a wonderful way,
grant, we pray,
that with prompt devotion and eager faith
the Christian people may hasten
toward the solemn celebrations to come.
Through our Lord Jesus Christ, your Son,
who lives and reigns with you in the unity of the Holy Spirit,
one God, for ever and ever.

The Creed is said.

Prayer over the Offerings

We place before you with joy these offerings,
which bring eternal remedy, O Lord,
praying that we may both faithfully revere them
and present them to you, as is fitting,
for the salvation of all the world.
Through Christ our Lord.

When the Gospel of the Man Born Blind is not read, Preface I or II of Lent, pp. **000–000**, is used.

Preface: The Man Born Blind, p. **000**.

Communion Antiphon

When the Gospel of the Man Born Blind is read: Cf. Jn 9: 11, 38

**The Lord anointed my eyes: I went, I washed,
I saw and I believed in God.**

When the Gospel of the Prodigal Son is read: Lk 15: 32

**You must rejoice, my son,
for your brother was dead and has come to life;
he was lost and is found.**

When another Gospel is read: Cf. Ps 122 (121): 3–4

**Jerusalem is built as a city bonded as one together.
It is there that the tribes go up, the tribes of the Lord,
to praise the name of the Lord.**

Prayer after Communion

**O God, who enlighten everyone who comes into this world,
illuminate our hearts, we pray,
with the splendor of your grace,
that we may always ponder
what is worthy and pleasing to your majesty
and love you in all sincerity.
Through Christ our Lord.**

Prayer over the People

**Look upon those who call to you, O Lord,
and sustain the weak;
give life by your unfailing light
to those who walk in the shadow of death,
and bring those rescued by your mercy from every evil
to reach the highest good.
Through Christ our Lord.**

FIFTH SUNDAY OF LENT

On this Sunday is celebrated the third scrutiny in preparation for the Baptism of the catechumens who are to be admitted to the Sacraments of Christian Initiation at the Easter Vigil, using the proper prayers and intercessions as given below, pp. **000–000**.

Entrance Antiphon   Cf. Ps 43 (42): 1–2

Give me justice, O God,
and plead my cause against a nation that is faithless.
From the deceitful and cunning rescue me,
for you, O God, are my strength.

The Gloria in excelsis (Glory to God in the highest) is not said.

Collect

By your help, we beseech you, Lord our God,
may we walk eagerly in that same charity
with which, out of love for the world,
your Son handed himself over to death.
Through our Lord Jesus Christ, your Son,
who lives and reigns with you in the unity of the Holy Spirit,
one God, for ever and ever.

The Creed is said.

Prayer over the Offerings

Hear us, almighty God,
and, having instilled in your servants
the teachings of the Christian faith,
graciously purify them
by the working of this sacrifice.
Through Christ our Lord.

When the Gospel of Lazarus is not read, Preface I or II of Lent, pp. **000–000**, is used.

Preface: Lazarus, p. **000**.

Communion Antiphon

When the Gospel of Lazarus is read: Cf. Jn 11: 26
Everyone who lives and believes in me
will not die for ever, says the Lord.

When the Gospel of the Adulterous Woman is read: Jn 8: 10–11
Has no one condemned you, woman? No one, Lord.
Neither shall I condemn you. From now on, sin no more.

When another Gospel is read: Jn 12: 24
Amen, Amen I say to you: Unless a grain of wheat
falls to the ground and dies, it remains a single grain.
But if it dies, it bears much fruit.

Prayer after Communion

We pray, almighty God,
that we may always be counted among the members of Christ,
in whose Body and Blood we have communion.
Who lives and reigns for ever and ever.

Prayer over the People

Bless, O Lord, your people,
who long for the gift of your mercy,
and grant that what, at your prompting, they desire,
they may receive by your generous gift.
Through Christ our Lord.

Notes

EASTER TIME

EASTER SUNDAY
OF THE RESURRECTION OF THE LORD

The fifty days from the Sunday of the Resurrection to Pentecost Sunday are celebrated in joy and exultation as one feast day, indeed as one "great Sunday." These are the days above all others in which the Alleluia is sung. (UNLYC, no. 22)

At Mass during the Day

71. Entrance Antiphon   Cf. Ps 139 (138): 18, 5–6

I have risen, and I am with you still, alleluia.
You have laid your hand upon me, alleluia.
Too wonderful for me, this knowledge, alleluia, alleluia.

Or: Lk 24: 34; cf. Rev 1: 6

The Lord is truly risen, alleluia.
To him be glory and power
for all the ages of eternity, alleluia, alleluia.

The Gloria in excelsis (Glory to God in the highest) is said.

72. Collect

O God, who on this day,
through your Only Begotten Son,
have conquered death
and unlocked for us the path to eternity,
grant, we pray, that we who keep
the solemnity of the Lord's Resurrection
may, through the renewal brought by your Spirit,
rise up in the light of life.
Through our Lord Jesus Christ, your Son,
who lives and reigns with you in the unity of the Holy Spirit,
one God, for ever and ever.

The Creed is said.

However, in Easter Sunday Masses which are celebrated with a congregation, the rite of the renewal of baptismal promises may take place after the Homily, according to the text used at the Easter Vigil (p. **000**). In that case the Creed is omitted.

73. Prayer over the Offerings

Exultant with paschal gladness, O Lord,
we offer the sacrifice
by which your Church
is wondrously reborn and nourished.
Through Christ our Lord.

74. Preface I of Easter, The Paschal Mystery, pp. **000–000**.

When the Roman Canon is used, the proper forms of the **Communicantes** (**In communion with those**) and **Hanc igitur** (**Therefore, Lord, we pray**) are said.

75. Communion Antiphon   1 Cor 5: 7-8

Christ our Passover has been sacrificed, alleluia;
therefore let us keep the feast with the unleavened bread
of purity and truth, alleluia, alleluia.

76. Prayer after Communion

**Look upon your Church, O God,
with unfailing love and favor,
so that, renewed by the paschal mysteries,
she may come to the glory of the resurrection.
Through Christ our Lord.**

77.   To impart the blessing at the end of Mass, the Priest may appropriately use the formula of Solemn Blessing for the Mass of the Easter Vigil, p. 000.

78.   For the dismissal of the people, there is sung (as above no. 69) or said:

Go forth, the Mass is ended, alleluia, alleluia.

Or:

**Go in peace, alleluia, alleluia.
℟. Thanks be to God, alleluia, alleluia.**

SECOND SUNDAY OF EASTER
(or of Divine Mercy)

Entrance Antiphon
1 Pt 2:2

Like newborn infants, you must long for the pure, spiritual milk,
that in him you may grow to salvation, alleluia.

Or:
4 Esdr 2:36–37

Receive the joy of your glory, giving thanks to God,
who has called you into the heavenly kingdom, alleluia.

The Gloria in excelsis (Glory to God in the highest) is said.

Collect

God of everlasting mercy,
who, in the very recurrence of the paschal feast
kindle the faith of the people you have made your own,
increase, we pray, the grace you have bestowed,
that all may grasp and rightly understand
in what font they have been washed,
by whose Spirit they have been reborn,
by whose Blood they have been redeemed.
Through our Lord Jesus Christ, your Son,
who lives and reigns with you in the unity of the Holy Spirit,
one God, for ever and ever.

The Creed is said.

Prayer over the Offerings

Accept, O Lord, we pray,
the oblations of your people
(and of those you have brought to new birth),
that, renewed by confession of your name and by Baptism,
they may attain unending happiness.
Through Christ our Lord.

Preface I of Easter (...on this day above all...), p. 000.

When the Roman Canon is used, the proper forms of the Communicantes (In communion with those) and Hanc igitur (Therefore, Lord, we pray) are said.

Notes

Communion Antiphon

Cf. Jn 20:27

Bring your hand and feel the place of the nails,
and do not be unbelieving but believing, alleluia.

Prayer after Communion

Grant, we pray, almighty God,
that our reception of this paschal Sacrament
may have a continuing effect
in our minds and hearts.
Through Christ our Lord.

A formula of Solemn Blessing, p. 000, may be used.

For the dismissal of the people, there is sung (as above, p. 000) or said: Go forth, the
Mass is ended, alleluia, alleluia. Or: Go in peace, alleluia, alleluia. The people respond:
Thanks be to God, alleluia, alleluia.

THIRD SUNDAY OF EASTER

Entrance Antiphon
Cf. Ps 66 (65): 1–2

Cry out with joy to God, all the earth;
O sing to the glory of his name.
O render him glorious praise, alleluia.

The Gloria in excelsis (Glory to God in the highest) is said.

Collect

May your people exult for ever, O God,
in renewed youthfulness of spirit,
so that, rejoicing now in the restored glory of our adoption,
we may look forward in confident hope
to the rejoicing of the day of resurrection.
Through our Lord Jesus Christ, your Son,
who lives and reigns with you in the unity of the Holy Spirit,
one God, for ever and ever.

The Creed is said.

Prayer over the Offerings

Receive, O Lord, we pray,
these offerings of your exultant Church,
and, as you have given her cause for such great gladness,
grant also that the gifts we bring
may bear fruit in perpetual happiness.
Through Christ our Lord.

Preface of Easter, pp. 000–000.

Communion Antiphon   Lk 24:35

**The disciples recognized the Lord Jesus
in the breaking of the bread, alleluia.**

Optional for Year B: Lk 24:46–47

**The Christ had to suffer and on the third day rise from the dead;
in his name repentance and remission of sins
must be preached to all the nations, alleluia.**

Optional for Year C: Cf. Jn 21:12–13

**Jesus said to his disciples: Come and eat.
And he took bread and gave it to them, alleluia.**

Prayer after Communion

**Look with kindness upon your people, O Lord,
and grant, we pray,
that those you were pleased to renew by eternal mysteries
may attain in their flesh
the incorruptible glory of the resurrection.
Through Christ our Lord.**

A formula of Solemn Blessing, p. **000**, may be used.

FOURTH SUNDAY OF EASTER

Entrance Antiphon

Cf. Ps 33 (32): 5–6

The merciful love of the Lord fills the earth;
by the word of the Lord the heavens were made, alleluia.

The Gloria in excelsis (Glory to God in the highest) is said.

Collect

Almighty ever-living God,
lead us to a share in the joys of heaven,
so that the humble flock may reach
where the brave Shepherd has gone before.
Who lives and reigns with you in the unity of the Holy Spirit,
one God, for ever and ever.

The Creed is said.

Prayer over the Offerings

Grant, we pray, O Lord,
that we may always find delight in these paschal mysteries,
so that the renewal constantly at work within us
may be the cause of our unending joy.
Through Christ our Lord.

Preface of Easter, pp. 000–000.

Communion Antiphon

The Good Shepherd has risen,
who laid down his life for his sheep
and willingly died for his flock, alleluia.

Prayer after Communion

Look upon your flock, kind Shepherd,
and be pleased to settle in eternal pastures
the sheep you have redeemed
by the Precious Blood of your Son.
Who lives and reigns for ever and ever.

A formula of Solemn Blessing, p. 000, may be used.

FIFTH SUNDAY OF EASTER

Entrance Antiphon   Cf. Ps 98 (97): 1–2

O sing a new song to the Lord,
for he has worked wonders;
in the sight of the nations
he has shown his deliverance, alleluia.

The Gloria in excelsis (Glory to God in the highest) is said.

Collect

Almighty ever-living God,
constantly accomplish the Paschal Mystery within us,
that those you were pleased to make new in Holy Baptism,
may, under your protective care, bear much fruit
and come to the joys of life eternal.
Through our Lord Jesus Christ, your Son,
who lives and reigns with you in the unity of the Holy Spirit,
one God, for ever and ever.

The Creed is said.

Prayer over the Offerings

O God, who by the wonderful exchange effected in this sacrifice
have made us partakers of the one supreme Godhead,
grant, we pray,
that, as we have come to know your truth,
we may make it ours by a worthy way of life.
Through Christ our Lord.

Preface of Easter, pp. 000–000.

Communion Antiphon   Cf. Jn 15: 1, 5

I am the true vine and you are the branches, says the Lord.
Whoever remains in me, and I in him, bears fruit in plenty, alleluia.

Prayer after Communion

Graciously be present to your people, we pray, O Lord,
and lead those you have imbued with heavenly mysteries
to pass from former ways to newness of life.
Through Christ our Lord.

A formula of Solemn Blessing, p. 000, may be used.

SIXTH SUNDAY OF EASTER

Entrance Antiphon   Cf. Is 48:20
Proclaim a joyful sound and let it be heard;
proclaim to the ends of the earth:
The Lord has freed his people, alleluia.

The Gloria in excelsis (Glory to God in the highest) is said.

Collect
Grant, almighty God,
that we may celebrate with heartfelt devotion these days of joy,
which we keep in honor of the risen Lord,
and that what we relive in remembrance
we may always hold to in what we do.
Through our Lord Jesus Christ, your Son,
who lives and reigns with you in the unity of the Holy Spirit,
one God, for ever and ever.

The Creed is said.

Prayer over the Offerings
May our prayers rise up to you, O Lord,
together with the sacrificial offerings,
so that, purified by your graciousness,
we may be conformed to the mysteries of your mighty love.
Through Christ our Lord.

Preface of Easter, pp. 000–000.

Communion Antiphon   Jn 14:15–16
If you love me, keep my commandments, says the Lord,
and I will ask the Father and he will send you another Paraclete,
to abide with you for ever, alleluia.

Prayer after Communion
Almighty ever-living God,
who restore us to eternal life in the Resurrection of Christ,
increase in us, we pray, the fruits of this paschal Sacrament
and pour into our hearts the strength of this saving food.
Through Christ our Lord.

A formula of Solemn Blessing, p.000, may be used.

SEVENTH SUNDAY OF EASTER

Entrance Antiphon   Cf. Ps 27 (26): 7–9

O Lord, hear my voice, for I have called to you;
of you my heart has spoken: Seek his face;
hide not your face from me, alleluia.

The Gloria in excelsis (Glory to God in the highest) is said.

Collect

Graciously hear our supplications, O Lord,
so that we, who believe that the Savior of the human race
is with you in your glory,
may experience, as he promised,
until the end of the world,
his abiding presence among us.
Who lives and reigns with you in the unity of the Holy Spirit,
one God, for ever and ever.

The Creed is said.

Prayer over the Offerings

Accept, O Lord, the prayers of your faithful
with the sacrificial offerings,
that through these acts of devotedness
we may pass over to the glory of heaven.
Through Christ our Lord.

Preface of Easter, or of the Ascension, pp. **000–000**.

Communion Antiphon   Jn 17:22

Father, I pray that they may be one
as we also are one, alleluia.

Prayer after Communion

Hear us, O God our Savior,
and grant us confidence,
that through these sacred mysteries
there will be accomplished in the body of the whole Church
what has already come to pass in Christ her Head.
Who lives and reigns for ever and ever.

A formula of Solemn Blessing, p. **000**, may be used.

PROPER OF SAINTS

NOVEMBER

November 1
ALL SAINTS
Solemnity

Entrance Antiphon

Let us all rejoice in the Lord,
as we celebrate the feast day in honor of all the Saints,
at whose festival the Angels rejoice
and praise the Son of God.

The Gloria in excelsis (Glory to God in the highest) is said.

Collect

Almighty ever-living God,
by whose gift we venerate in one celebration
the merits of all the Saints,
bestow on us, we pray,
through the prayers of so many intercessors,
an abundance of the reconciliation with you
for which we earnestly long.
Through our Lord Jesus Christ, your Son,
who lives and reigns with you in the unity of the Holy Spirit,
one God, for ever and ever.

The Creed is said.

Prayer over the Offerings

May these offerings we bring in honor of all the Saints
be pleasing to you, O Lord,
and grant that, just as we believe the Saints
to be already assured of immortality,
so we may experience their concern for our salvation.
Through Christ our Lord.

Preface: The glory of Jerusalem, our mother.

℣. The Lord be with you.
℞. And with your spirit.

℣. Lift up your hearts.
℞. We lift them up to the Lord.

℣. Let us give thanks to the Lord our God.
℞. It is right and just.

It is truly right and just, our duty and our salvation,
always and everywhere to give you thanks,
Lord, holy Father, almighty and eternal God.

For today by your gift we celebrate the festival of your city,
the heavenly Jerusalem, our mother,
where the great array of our brothers and sisters
already gives you eternal praise.

Towards her, we eagerly hasten, as pilgrims advancing by faith,
rejoicing in the glory bestowed upon those exalted members of the Church
through whom you give us, in our frailty, both strength and good example.
And so, we glorify you with the multitude of Saints and Angels,
as with one voice of praise we acclaim:

Holy, Holy, Holy Lord God of hosts…

Communion Antiphon   Mt 5: 8–10

Blessed are the clean of heart, for they shall see God.
Blessed are the peacemakers,
for they shall be called children of God.
Blessed are they who are persecuted for the sake of righteousness,
for theirs is the kingdom of heaven.

Prayer after Communion

As we adore you, O God, who alone are holy
and wonderful in all your Saints,
we implore your grace,
so that, coming to perfect holiness in the fullness of your love,
we may pass from this pilgrim table
to the banquet of our heavenly homeland.
Through Christ our Lord.

The Solemn Blessing formula, pp. **000–000**, may be used.

For the Votive Mass of All Saints, see p. **000**.

November 2

THE COMMEMORATION
OF ALL THE FAITHFUL DEPARTED
(All Souls' Day)

The Masses that follow may be used at the discretion of the celebrant.*

Even when 2 November falls on a Sunday, the Mass celebrated is that of the Commemoration of All the Faithful Departed.

1

Entrance Antiphon   Cf. 1 Thes 4:14; 1 Cor 15:22

**Just as Jesus died and has risen again,
so through Jesus God will bring with him
those who have fallen asleep;
and as in Adam all die,
so also in Christ will all be brought to life.**

Collect

**Listen kindly to our prayers, O Lord,
and, as our faith in your Son,
raised from the dead, is deepened,
so may our hope of resurrection for your departed servants
also find new strength.
Through our Lord Jesus Christ, your Son,
who lives and reigns with you in the unity of the Holy Spirit,
one God, for ever and ever.**

Prayer over the Offerings

**Look favorably on our offerings, O Lord,
so that your departed servants
may be taken up into glory with your Son,
in whose great mystery of love we are all united.
Who lives and reigns for ever and ever.**

Preface for the Dead, pp. 000–000.

_____

   * On this day, any Priest may celebrate three Masses, observing, nevertheless, what was established by Benedict XV in the Apostolic Constitution, *Incruentum Altaris Sacrificium*, 10 August 1915: *Acta Apostolicæ Sedis* 7 (1915) pp. 401–404.

Communion Antiphon   Cf. Jn 11:25–26

I am the Resurrection and the Life, says the Lord.
Whoever believes in me, even though he dies, will live,
and everyone who lives and believes in me will not die for ever.

Prayer after Communion

Grant we pray, O Lord, that your departed servants,
for whom we have celebrated this paschal Sacrament,
may pass over to a dwelling place of light and peace.
Through Christ our Lord.

The Solemn Blessing formula, pp. **000–000**, may be used.

2

Entrance Antiphon   Cf. 4 Esdr 2:34–35

Eternal rest grant unto them, O Lord,
and let perpetual light shine upon them.

Collect

O God, glory of the faithful and life of the just,
by the Death and Resurrection of whose Son
we have been redeemed,
look mercifully on your departed servants,
that, just as they professed the mystery of our resurrection,
so they may merit to receive the joys of eternal happiness.
Through our Lord Jesus Christ, your Son,
who lives and reigns with you in the unity of the Holy Spirit,
one God, for ever and ever.

Prayer over the Offerings

Almighty and merciful God,
by means of these sacrificial offerings
wash away, we pray, in the Blood of Christ,
the sins of your departed servants,
for you purify unceasingly by your merciful forgiveness
those you once cleansed in the waters of Baptism.
Through Christ our Lord.

Preface for the Dead, pp. **000–000**.

Communion Antiphon

Cf. 4 Esdr 2:35, 34

Let perpetual light shine upon them, O Lord,
with your Saints for ever, for you are merciful.

Prayer after Communion

Having received the Sacrament of your Only Begotten Son,
who was sacrificed for us and rose in glory,
we humbly implore you, O Lord,
for your departed servants,
that, cleansed by the paschal mysteries,
they may glory in the gift of the resurrection to come.
Through Christ our Lord.

The Solemn Blessing formula, p.000, may be used.

3

Entrance Antiphon

Cf. Rom 8:11

God, who raised Jesus from the dead,
will give life also to your mortal bodies,
through his Spirit that dwells in you.

Collect

O God, who willed that your Only Begotten Son,
having conquered death,
should pass over into the realm of heaven,
grant, we pray, to your departed servants
that, with the mortality of this life overcome,
they may gaze eternally on you,
their Creator and Redeemer.
Through our Lord Jesus Christ, your Son,
who lives and reigns with you in the unity of the Holy Spirit,
one God, for ever and ever.

Prayer over the Offerings

Receive, Lord, in your kindness,
the sacrificial offering we make
for all your servants who sleep in Christ,
that, set free from the bonds of death
by this singular sacrifice,
they may merit eternal life.
Through Christ our Lord.

Preface for the Dead, pp. 000–000.

Communion Antiphon   Cf. Phil 3:20–21

We await a savior, the Lord Jesus Christ,
who will change our mortal bodies,
to conform with his glorified body.

Prayer after Communion

Through these sacrificial gifts
which we have received, O Lord,
bestow on your departed servants your great mercy
and, to those you have endowed with the grace of Baptism,
grant also the fullness of eternal joy.
Through Christ our Lord.

The Solemn Blessing formula, p. 000, may be used.

November 3

Saint Martin de Porres, Religious

From the Common of Holy Men and Women: For Religious (p.000).

Collect

**O God, who led Saint Martin de Porres
by the path of humility to heavenly glory,
grant that we may so follow his radiant example in this life
as to merit to be exalted with him in heaven.
Through our Lord Jesus Christ, your Son,
who lives and reigns with you in the unity of the Holy Spirit,
one God, for ever and ever.**

November 4
Saint Charles Borromeo, Bishop
Memorial

From the Common of Pastors: For a Bishop (p.000).

Collect

Preserve in the midst of your people,
we ask, O Lord, the spirit with which you filled
the Bishop Saint Charles Borromeo,
that your Church may be constantly renewed
and, by conforming herself to the likeness of Christ,
may show his face to the world.
Who lives and reigns with you in the unity of the Holy Spirit,
one God, for ever and ever.

Prayer over the Offerings

Look, O Lord, upon the offering placed on your altar
in commemoration of Saint Charles,
and grant by the power of this sacrifice
that, as you made him an attentive pastor,
outstanding in the merit of his virtues,
so you may make us abound in good fruit by our works.
Through Christ our Lord.

Prayer after Communion

May the sacred mysteries of which we have partaken,
O Lord, we pray, give us that determination
which made Saint Charles faithful in ministry
and fervent in charity.
Through Christ our Lord.

November 9

THE DEDICATION
OF THE LATERAN BASILICA

Feast

In the basilica itself, the Mass of the Common of the Dedication of a Church is used (p. 000).

Entrance Antiphon   Cf. Rev 21:2

I saw the holy city, a new Jerusalem,
coming down out of heaven from God,
prepared like a bride adorned for her husband.

Or: Cf. Rev 21:3

Behold God's dwelling with the human race.
He will dwell with them and they will be his people,
and God himself with them will be their God.

The Gloria in excelsis (Glory to God in the highest) is said.

Collect

O God, who from living and chosen stones
prepare an eternal dwelling for your majesty,
increase in your Church the spirit of grace you have bestowed,
so that by new growth your faithful people
may build up the heavenly Jerusalem.
Through our Lord Jesus Christ, your Son,
who lives and reigns with you in the unity of the Holy Spirit,
one God, for ever and ever.

Or:

O God, who were pleased to call your Church the Bride,
grant that the people that serves your name
may revere you, love you and follow you,
and may be led by you
to attain your promises in heaven.
Through our Lord Jesus Christ, your Son,
who lives and reigns with you in the unity of the Holy Spirit,
one God, for ever and ever.

When this Feast falls on a Sunday, the Creed is said.

Prayer over the Offerings
Accept, we pray, O Lord, the offering made here
and grant that by it those who seek your favor
may receive in this place
the power of the Sacraments
and the answer to their prayers.
Through Christ our Lord.

Preface: The mystery of the Church, the Bride of Christ and the Temple of the Spirit.
℣. The Lord be with you.
℟. And with your spirit.

℣. Lift up your hearts.
℟. We lift them up to the Lord.

℣. Let us give thanks to the Lord our God.
℟. It is right and just.

It is truly right and just, our duty and our salvation,
always and everywhere to give you thanks,
Lord, holy Father, almighty and eternal God.

For in your benevolence you are pleased
to dwell in this house of prayer
in order to perfect us as the temple of the Holy Spirit,
supported by the perpetual help of your grace
and resplendent with the glory of a life acceptable to you.

Year by year you sanctify the Church, the Bride of Christ,
foreshadowed in visible buildings,
so that, rejoicing as the mother of countless children,
she may be given her place in your heavenly glory.

And so, with all the Angels and Saints,
we praise you, as without end we acclaim:

Holy, Holy, Holy Lord God of hosts...

Communion Antiphon

Cf. 1 Pt 2:5

Be built up like living stones,
into a spiritual house, a holy priesthood.

Prayer after Communion

O God, who chose to foreshadow for us
the heavenly Jerusalem
through the sign of your Church on earth,
grant, we pray,
that, by our partaking of this Sacrament,
we may be made the temple of your grace
and may enter the dwelling place of your glory.
Through Christ our Lord.

The Solemn Blessing formula, pp. 000–000, may be used.

November 10

Saint Leo the Great, Pope and Doctor of the Church

Memorial

Entrance Antiphon   Cf. Sir 45:30
The Lord established for him a covenant of peace,
and made him the prince,
that he might have the dignity of the priesthood for ever.

Collect
O God, who never allow the gates of hell
to prevail against your Church,
firmly founded on the apostolic rock,
grant her, we pray,
that through the intercession of Pope Saint Leo,
she may stand firm in your truth
and know the protection of lasting peace.
Through our Lord Jesus Christ, your Son,
who lives and reigns with you in the unity of the Holy Spirit,
one God, for ever and ever.

Prayer over the Offerings
Through the offerings made here, we pray, O Lord,
graciously shed light on your Church,
so that your flock may everywhere prosper
and that under your governance
the shepherds may become pleasing to your name.
Through Christ our Lord.

Communion Antiphon

Mt 16: 16, 18

Peter said to Jesus:
You are the Christ, the Son of the living God.
And Jesus replied: You are Peter,
and upon this rock I will build my Church.

Prayer after Communion

Be pleased, O Lord, we pray,
to govern the Church you have nourished by this holy meal,
so that, firmly directed,
she may enjoy ever greater freedom
and persevere in integrity of religion.
Through Christ our Lord.

November 11
Saint Martin of Tours, Bishop
Memorial

Entrance Antiphon   Cf. 1 Sm 2:35

I shall raise up for myself a faithful priest
who will act in accord with my heart and my mind, says the Lord.

Collect

O God, who are glorified in the Bishop Saint Martin
both by his life and death,
make new, we pray,
the wonders of your grace in our hearts,
that neither death nor life
may separate us from your love.
Through our Lord Jesus Christ, your Son,
who lives and reigns with you in the unity of the Holy Spirit,
one God, for ever and ever.

Prayer over the Offerings

Sanctify these offerings, we pray, Lord God,
which we joyfully present in honor of Saint Martin,
so that through them our life may always be directed
whether in tribulation or in prosperity.
Through Christ our Lord.

Communion Antiphon   Cf. Mt 25:40

Amen, I say to you:
Whatever you did for one of the least of my brethren,
you did it for me, says the Lord.

Prayer after Communion

Grant to us who have been restored
by this Sacrament of unity, O Lord,
perfect harmony with your will in all things,
that, just as Saint Martin submitted himself entirely to you,
so we, too, may glory in being truly yours.
Through Christ our Lord.

November 12
Saint Josaphat, Bishop and Martyr
Memorial

Entrance Antiphon

Because of the Lord's covenant and the ancestral laws,
the Saints of God persevered in loving brotherhood,
for there was always one spirit in them, and one faith.

Collect

Stir up in your Church, we pray, O Lord,
the Spirit that filled Saint Josaphat
as he laid down his life for the sheep,
so that through his intercession
we, too, may be strengthened by the same Spirit
and not be afraid to lay down our life for others.
Through our Lord Jesus Christ, your Son,
who lives and reigns with you in the unity of the Holy Spirit,
one God, for ever and ever.

Prayer over the Offerings

Most merciful God,
pour out your blessing upon these offerings
and confirm us in the faith
that Saint Josaphat professed by the shedding of his blood.
Through Christ our Lord.

Communion Antiphon   Mt 10:39

Whoever loses his life for my sake,
will find it in eternity, say the Lord.

Prayer after Communion

May this heavenly table, O Lord,
bestow on us a spirit of fortitude and peace,
so that, following Saint Josaphat's example,
we may willingly spend our lives
working for the honor and unity of the Church.
Through Christ our Lord.

November 15

Saint Albert the Great, Bishop and Doctor of the Church

From the Common of Pastors: For a Bishop (p.**000**), or from the Common of Doctors of the Church (p.**000**).

Collect

**O God, who made the Bishop Saint Albert great
by his joining of human wisdom to divine faith,
grant, we pray, that we may so adhere to the truths he taught,
that through progress in learning
we may come to a deeper knowledge and love of you.
Through our Lord Jesus Christ, your Son,
who lives and reigns with you in the unity of the Holy Spirit,
one God, for ever and ever.**

November 16
Saint Margaret of Scotland

From the Common of Holy Men and Women: For Those Who Practiced Works of Mercy (p. 000).

Collect

O God, who made Saint Margaret of Scotland wonderful
in her outstanding charity towards the poor,
grant that through her intercession and example
we may reflect among all humanity
the image of your divine goodness.
Through our Lord Jesus Christ, your Son,
who lives and reigns with you in the unity of the Holy Spirit,
one God, for ever and ever.

Saint Gertrude, Virgin

From the Common of Virgins (p. 000), or from the Common of Holy Men and Women: For a Nun (p. 000).

Collect

O God, who prepared a delightful dwelling for yourself
in the heart of the Virgin Saint Gertrude,
graciously bring light, through her intercession,
to the darkness of our hearts,
that we may joyfully experience you present and at work within us.
Through our Lord Jesus Christ, your Son,
who lives and reigns with you in the unity of the Holy Spirit,
one God, for ever and ever.

November 17
Saint Elizabeth of Hungary, Religious
Memorial

From the Common of Holy Men and Women: For Those Who Practiced Works of Mercy (p. 000).

Collect

**O God, by whose gift Saint Elizabeth of Hungary
recognized and revered Christ in the poor,
grant, through her intercession,
that we may serve with unfailing charity
the needy and those afflicted.
Through our Lord Jesus Christ, your Son,
who lives and reigns with you in the unity of the Holy Spirit,
one God, for ever and ever.**

November 18

The Dedication of the Basilicas
of Saints Peter and Paul, Apostles

Entrance Antiphon

Cf. Ps 45 (44): 17–18

You will make them princes over all the earth;
they will remember your name through all generations.
Thus the peoples will praise you for ever, from age to age.

Collect

Defend your Church, O Lord,
by the protection of the holy Apostles,
that, as she received from them
the beginnings of her knowledge of things divine,
so through them she may receive,
even to the end of the world,
an increase in heavenly grace.
Through our Lord Jesus Christ, your Son,
who lives and reigns with you in the unity of the Holy Spirit,
one God, for ever and ever.

Prayer over the Offerings

As we bring you this offering of our service,
we beseech your mercy, Lord,
that the truth handed down to us
by the ministry of the Apostles Peter and Paul
may endure undefiled in our hearts.
Through Christ our Lord.

Preface of the Apostles, pp. 000–000.

Communion Antiphon   Cf. Jn 6:69, 70

O Lord, you have the words of eternal life,
and we have come to believe
that you are the Christ, the Son of God.

Prayer after Communion

May your people, we pray, O Lord,
nourished by the Bread of heaven,
rejoice in commemorating the Apostles Peter and Paul,
for it is through your gift
that we are governed under their patronage.
Through Christ our Lord.

November 21
The Presentation of the Blessed Virgin Mary
Memorial

From the Common of the Blessed Virgin Mary (p. 000).

Collect

As we venerate the glorious memory
of the most holy Virgin Mary,
grant, we pray, O Lord, through her intercession,
that we, too, may merit to receive
from the fullness of your grace.
Through our Lord Jesus Christ, your Son,
who lives and reigns with you in the unity of the Holy Spirit,
one God, for ever and ever.

November 22
Saint Cecilia, Virgin and Martyr
Memorial

From the Common of Martyrs: For a Virgin Martyr (p. 000), or from the Common of Virgins: For One Virgin (p. 000).

Collect

**O God, who gladden us each year
with the feast day of your handmaid Saint Cecilia,
grant, we pray,
that what has been devoutly handed down concerning her
may offer us examples to imitate
and proclaim the wonders worked in his servants
by Christ your Son.
Who lives and reigns with you in the unity of the Holy Spirit,
one God, for ever and ever.**

November 23

Saint Clement I, Pope and Martyr

From the Common of Martyrs: For One Martyr (p. 000), or from the Common of Pastors: For a Pope (p. 000).

Collect

Almighty ever-living God,
who are wonderful in the virtue of all your Saints,
grant us joy in the yearly commemoration of Saint Clement,
who, as a Martyr and High Priest of your Son,
bore out by his witness what he celebrated in mystery
and confirmed by example what he preached with his lips.
Through our Lord Jesus Christ, your Son,
who lives and reigns with you in the unity of the Holy Spirit,
one God, for ever and ever.

Saint Columban, Abbot

From the Common of Pastors: For Missionaries (p. 000), or from the Common of Holy Men and Women: For an Abbot (p. 000).

Collect

O God, who in Saint Columban
wonderfully joined the work of evangelization
to zeal for the monastic life,
grant, we pray,
that through his intercession and example
we may strive to seek you above all things
and to bring increase to your faithful people.
Through our Lord Jesus Christ, your Son,
who lives and reigns with you in the unity of the Holy Spirit,
one God, for ever and ever.

November 24

Saint Andrew Dũng-Lạc, Priest,
and Companions, Martyrs

Memorial

Entrance Antiphon   Cf. Gal 6:14; cf. 1 Cor 1:18

May we never boast, except in the Cross of our Lord Jesus Christ.
For the word of the Cross is the power of God
to us who have been saved.

Collect

O God, source and origin of all fatherhood,
who kept the Martyrs Saint Andrew Dũng-Lạc and his companions
faithful to the Cross of your Son,
even to the shedding of their blood,
grant, through their intercession,
that, spreading your love among our brothers and sisters,
we may be your children both in name and in truth.
Through our Lord Jesus Christ, your Son,
who lives and reigns with you in the unity of the Holy Spirit,
one God, for ever and ever.

Prayer over the Offerings

Receive, O holy Father, the offerings we bring
as we venerate the passion of the holy Martyrs,
so that amid the trials of this life
we may always be found faithful
and may offer ourselves to you
as an acceptable sacrifice.
Through Christ our Lord.

Communion Antiphon

Mt 5:10

Blessed are they who are persecuted for the sake of righteousness,
for theirs is the kingdom of heaven.

Prayer after Communion

Renewed by the one Bread
as we commemorate the holy Martyrs,
we humbly beseech you, O Lord,
that, abiding as one in your love,
we may merit by endurance an eternal prize.
Through Christ our Lord.

November 25

Saint Catherine of Alexandria, Virgin and Martyr

From the Common of Martyrs: For a Virgin Martyr (p. 000), or from the Common of Virgins: For One Virgin (p. 000).

Collect

Almighty ever-living God,
who gave Saint Catherine of Alexandria to your people
as a Virgin and an invincible Martyr,
grant that through her intercession
we may be strengthened in faith and constancy
and spend ourselves without reserve
for the unity of the Church.
Through our Lord Jesus Christ, your Son,
who lives and reigns with you in the unity of the Holy Spirit,
one God, for ever and ever.

November 30
SAINT ANDREW, APOSTLE
Feast

Entrance Antiphon
Cf. Mt 4: 18–19

Beside the Sea of Galilee,
the Lord saw two brothers, Peter and Andrew,
and he said to them:
Come after me and I will make you fishers of men.

The Gloria in excelsis (Glory to God in the highest) is said.

Collect
We humbly implore your majesty, O Lord,
that, just as the blessed Apostle Andrew
was for your Church a preacher and pastor,
so he may be for us a constant intercessor before you.
Through our Lord Jesus Christ, your Son,
who lives and reigns with you in the unity of the Holy Spirit,
one God, for ever and ever.

Prayer over the Offerings
Grant us, almighty God, that through these offerings,
which we bring on the feast day of Saint Andrew,
we may please you by what we have brought
and be given life by what you have accepted.
Through Christ our Lord.

Preface of the Apostles, pp. 000–000.

Communion Antiphon
Cf. Jn 1: 41–42

Andrew told his brother Simon:
We have found the Messiah, the Christ,
and he brought him to Jesus.

Prayer after Communion
May communion in your Sacrament strengthen us, O Lord,
so that, by the example of the blessed Apostle Andrew
we, who carry in our body the Death of Christ,
may merit to live with him in glory.
Who lives and reigns for ever and ever.

The Solemn Blessing formula, pp. 000–000, may be used.

MASSES AND PRAYERS
FOR VARIOUS NEEDS
AND OCCASIONS

Since the liturgy of the Sacraments and Sacramentals has as its effect that for the faithful who are properly disposed almost every event in life is sanctified by the divine grace that flows from the Paschal Mystery (Cf. Second Ecumenical Council of the Vatican, Constitution on the Sacred Liturgy, *Sacrosanctum Concilium*, no. 61), and because the Eucharist is the Sacrament of Sacraments, the Missal provides examples of Mass formularies and orations that may be used in the various occasions of Christian life for the needs of the whole world or for the needs of the Church, whether universal or local. (GIRM, no. 368)

I. FOR HOLY CHURCH

1. FOR THE CHURCH

A

Entrance Antiphon   Cf. Eph 1:9–10
God has made known to us the mystery of his will,
to bring together all things in Christ,
all things in heaven and on earth in him.

Collect
O God, who in your wonderful providence
decreed that Christ's kingdom
should be extended throughout the earth
and that all should become partakers of his saving redemption,
grant, we pray, that your Church
may be the universal sacrament of salvation
and that Christ may be revealed to all
as the hope of the nations and their Savior.
Who lives and reigns with you in the unity of the Holy Spirit,
one God, for ever and ever.

Prayer over the Offerings
Look upon the offerings of the people consecrated to you,
O merciful God,
and, through the power of this Sacrament,
grant that the multitude of those who believe in you
may constantly be made a chosen race,
a royal priesthood, a holy nation, a people of your own.
Through Christ our Lord.

Preface VIII of the Sundays in Ordinary Time, p. 000.

Communion Antiphon   Rev 22:17, 20

The Spirit and the bride say: Come.
Amen. Come, Lord Jesus.

Prayer after Communion

O God, who constantly feed and strengthen the Church
with your Sacraments,
grant to us,
who have been nourished at the heavenly table,
that, by obeying your teachings of love,
we may become for the human family
a life-giving leaven and a means to salvation.
Through Christ our Lord.

B

Entrance Antiphon   Rev 7:9

I had a vision of a great multitude, which no one could count,
from every nation, race, people, and tongue.

Collect

O God, in the covenant of your Christ
you never cease to gather to yourself from all nations
a people growing together in unity through the Spirit;
grant, we pray, that your Church,
faithful to the mission entrusted to her,
may continually go forward with the human family
and always be the leaven and the soul of human society,
to renew it in Christ and transform it into the family of God.
Through our Lord Jesus Christ, your Son,
who lives and reigns with you in the unity of the Holy Spirit,
one God, for ever and ever.

Prayer over the Offerings

Receive with kindness the offerings we bring you, O Lord,
and grant that your Church,
which came forth from the side of Christ as he slept on the Cross,
may ever draw her holiness from participation in this mystery,
living by it always and responding worthily to her founder,
Jesus Christ our Lord.
Who lives and reigns for ever and ever.

Preface VIII of the Sundays in Ordinary Time, p.000.

Communion Antiphon   Jn 19:34

One of the soldiers opened his side with a lance,
and at once there came forth blood and water.

Or: Rev 7:12

Blessing and glory and wisdom and thanksgiving,
honor and power and might
be to our God for ever and ever. Amen.

Prayer after Communion

Nourished by the Sacrament of your Son,
we implore you, Lord,
to make fruitful the work of your Church,
for by it you constantly reveal
the fullness of the mystery of salvation to the poor,
whom you have called to an honored place in your eternal Kingdom.
Through Christ our Lord.

C

Entrance Antiphon   Mt 18:20

Where two or three are gathered together in my name,
there am I in the midst of them.

Or: Rom 12:5

Though many, we are one body in Christ
and individually parts of one another.

Collect

Grant, we pray, almighty God,
that your Church may always remain that holy people,
formed as one by the unity of Father, Son and Holy Spirit,
which manifests to the world
the Sacrament of your holiness and unity
and leads it to the perfection of your charity.
Through our Lord Jesus Christ, your Son,
who lives and reigns with you in the unity of the Holy Spirit,
one God, for ever and ever.

Prayer over the Offerings

Celebrating the memorial of your Son's boundless love,
we humbly beseech you, O Lord,
that through the ministry of your Church
the fruits of his saving work
may advance the salvation of all the world.
Through Christ our Lord.

Preface for the Unity of Christians, pp. 0000–0000.

Communion Antiphon   Cf. 1 Cor 10:17

Though many, we are one bread, one body,
for we all partake of the one Bread and one Chalice.

Prayer after Communion

O God, who by this wonderful Sacrament
give courage and comfort to the Church,
grant that through these holy gifts
your people may hold fast to Christ,
so that, by the tasks they carry out in this present age,
they may in freedom build up your eternal Kingdom.
Through Christ our Lord.

D

Entrance Antiphon   Cf. Jn 17:20–21

Father, I pray for those who will believe in me,
that they may be one in us,
so that the world may believe it was you who sent me.

Collect

Almighty ever-living God,
who in Christ revealed your glory to all the nations,
watch over the works of your mercy,
that holy Church, spread throughout the whole world,
may persevere with steadfast faith in confessing your name.
Through our Lord Jesus Christ, your Son,
who lives and reigns with you in the unity of the Holy Spirit,
one God, for ever and ever.

Prayer over the Offerings

O God, who constantly sanctify your Church
through the same sacrifice by which you have made her clean,
grant that, united to Christ her Head,
she may offer herself to you with him
and be united with you in purity of will.
Through Christ our Lord.

Preface VIII of the Sundays in Ordinary Time, p. 000.

Communion Antiphon   Jn 15:5

Whoever remains in me and I in him bears fruit in plenty,
because without me you can do nothing, says the Lord.

Prayer after Communion

Be pleased, O Lord, we pray,
to govern the Church you have nourished by this holy meal,
so that, firmly directed,
she may enjoy ever greater freedom
and persevere in integrity of religion.
Through Christ our Lord.

E
For the Particular Church

Entrance Antiphon   Rev 1:5–6

To Jesus Christ who loves us
and has washed us clean of our sins by his Blood,
who has made us into a kingdom, priests for his God and Father.
To him be glory and power for ever and ever. Amen.

Collect

O God, who in each pilgrim Church throughout the world
make visible the one, holy, catholic and apostolic Church,
graciously grant
that your faithful may be so united to their shepherd
and gathered together in the Holy Spirit
through the Gospel and the Eucharist,
as to worthily embody the universality of your people
and become a sign and instrument in the world of the presence of Christ.
Who lives and reigns with you in the unity of the Holy Spirit,
one God, for ever and ever.

Prayer over the Offerings

**Celebrating the memorial of your Son's boundless love,
we humbly beseech you, O Lord,
that through the ministry of your Church
the fruits of his saving work
may advance the salvation of all the world.
Through Christ our Lord.**

Preface VIII of the Sundays in Ordinary Time, p. 000.

Communion Antiphon   Rev 3:20

Behold, I stand at the door and knock, says the Lord.
If anyone hears my voice and opens the door to me,
I will enter his house and dine with him, and he with me.

Prayer after Communion

**In this your Church, O Lord,
may integrity of faith, holiness of life,
fraternal charity and pure religion
flourish and abide until the end,
and, as you do not fail to feed her
with the Body of your Son and with your word,
so also never cease, we pray,
to guide her under your protection.
Through Christ our Lord.**

Notes

VOTIVE MASSES

Votive Masses of the mysteries of the Lord or in honor of the Blessed Virgin Mary or of the Angels or of any given Saint or of all the Saints may be said in response to the devotion of the faithful on weekdays in Ordinary Time, even if an optional memorial occurs. However, it is not permitted to celebrate as Votive Masses those that refer to mysteries related to events in the life of the Lord or of the Blessed Virgin Mary, with the exception of the Mass of the Immaculate Conception, since their celebration is an integral part of the course of the liturgical year. (GIRM, no. 375)

13. SAINT JOSEPH

In this Mass, the color white is used.

Entrance Antiphon   Cf. Lk 12:42
Behold, a faithful and prudent steward,
whom the Lord set over his household.

Collect
O God, who in your inexpressible providence
were pleased to choose Saint Joseph
as spouse of the most holy Mother of your Son,
grant, we pray,
that we, who revere him as our protector on earth,
may be worthy of his heavenly intercession.
Through our Lord Jesus Christ, your Son,
who lives and reigns with you in the unity of the Holy Spirit,
one God, for ever and ever.

Prayer over the Offerings
As we prepare to offer the sacrifice of praise, O holy Father,
we humbly ask to be sustained in our service
by the prayers of Saint Joseph,
whom you called to watch like a father on earth
over your Only Begotten Son.
Who lives and reigns for ever and ever.

Preface: The mission of Saint Joseph.

℣.   The Lord be with you.
℟.   And with your spirit.

℣.   Lift up your hearts.
℟.   We lift them up to the Lord.

℣.   Let us give thanks to the Lord our God.
℟.   It is right and just.

It is truly right and just, our duty and our salvation,
always and everywhere to give you thanks,
Lord, holy Father, almighty and eternal God,
and, in honoring Saint Joseph,
to give you fitting praise,
to glorify you and bless you.

For this just man was given by you
as spouse to the Virgin Mother of God
and set as a wise and faithful servant
in charge of your household,
to watch like a father over your Only Begotten Son,
who was conceived by the overshadowing of the Holy Spirit,
our Lord Jesus Christ.

Through him the Angels praise your majesty,
Dominions adore and Powers tremble before you.
Heaven and the Virtues of heaven and the blessed Seraphim
worship together with exultation.
May our voices, we pray, join with theirs
in humble praise, as we acclaim:

Holy, Holy, Holy Lord God of hosts...

Communion Antiphon   Mt 25:21

Well done, good and faithful servant;
come, share your master's joy.

Prayer after Communion

Restored by these life-giving Sacraments, Lord,
may we live for you always in justice and holiness,
helped by the example and intercession of Saint Joseph,
who in carrying out your great mysteries
served you as a man just and obedient.
Through Christ our Lord.

If appropriate, the Mass of the Solemnity, as on 19 March (p. 000), or of Saint Joseph the Worker, as on 1 May (p. 000), may also be said.